Worship Planning
Resources for
Every Sunday of the Year

The Abingdon
Worship Annual

2024

Edited by

Mary Scifres
and B. J. Beu

Abingdon Press / Nashville

THE ABINGDON WORSHIP ANNUAL 2024:
WORSHIP PLANNING RESOURCES
FOR EVERY SUNDAY OF THE YEAR

Copyright © 2023 by Abingdon Press

ISBN 978-1-7910-2704-9

MANUFACTURED IN THE UNITED STATES OF AMERICA

Contents

April

May

June

July

August

September

October

November

December

Introduction

Planning Virtual Worship— Pandemic or Not!

Until the global pandemic of 2020, very few of our readers had been planning worship for the virtual world. Some livestreamed or recorded worship services for homebound members, but very few put much thought into those virtual options in their creative thinking and planning. Now, almost all of us do. With that in mind, B. J. and I offer some insights and ideas to you, gleaned from your colleagues around the world.

Adapting Liturgy for Online Worship

Contained in these pages, you will find carefully and caringly crafted prayers and readings, along with theme ideas and centering words to help you and your congregation focus each week as you worship together. When worshiping online, we have all learned that some of our former traditions don't work as well in the virtual world. For responsive readings, inviting two leaders to read back and forth rather than one reader awaiting a congregation's unison response can be much more effective in livestream or video conference worship gatherings. Similarly, unison readings and singing are not that effective online due to the different timing. Instead, we encourage single readers—preferably various laypeople throughout the church year—to lead those formerly "unison" moments while others are encouraged to read along quietly, silently, or aloud with one another in their homes (while being "muted" online). If live streaming, intentionally add a moment of pause before and after any unison "in person" moments for the time delay that live streamers often experience as they worship from other locations. The moment of pause helps unify both congregations, while also allowing the gentle breath of the Holy Spirit to breathe a pause into our worshiping rhythm. Feel free to share the prayers and readings from within these pages not only online, but even in weekly e-newsletters or devotionals. Note the copyright and authorship, and then share with your people in creative ways to nourish their spiritual journeys. Let us know if you have questions about ways to innovate your use of liturgy and worship words, as we want to support and strengthen your ministry and that of your congregations.

Versions of Virtual Worship

There are many ways of worshiping together, whether worshiping in our homes, outdoors, in church buildings, or some combination thereof. For years, homebound and traveling church members have yearned to stay connected with their church families. Now, almost all of us have developed methods for staying connected through our computers, tablets, and phones. We hope you will continue connecting in these virtual ways, even when the dangers of a pandemic have passed. The more we can connect without regard to geography, the more inclusive our worship services and congregational relationships can be. Imagine how much joy we bring our homebound "visitors" when they stream worship right into their living rooms and assisted-living apartments. To stay "connected" in the past, my homebound grandmother had to rely on copies of *The Upper Room* and visits from her pastor. Now, all who can't attend Sunday worship can stay connected with your congregation, thanks to modern technology and the church's amazing willingness and ability to adapt in 2023!

As the pandemic spread around our globe, we watched colleagues without the ability to live stream create amazing possibilities from their smartphones, camcorders, and tablets. The following methods categorize some of the ways you have made virtual worship possible for your people.

1. Pre-recorded worship filmed in "one take"— weekly sermons, musical offerings, or even midweek devotions.

2. Pre-recorded worship filmed separately in various segments from multiple leaders and locations—distributed as individual elements or edited into a complete recorded worship service.

3. Pre-recorded musical offerings filmed from multiple participants and locations—edited into a virtual choir or ensemble.

4. Livestreamed sermons, meditations, or devotions.

5. Livestreamed worship services, inclusive of sermon, music, and liturgy.

6. Video-conference worship, using a service like Zoom, to allow for interaction and fellowship in the worship experience.

We applaud you for creating such beautiful worship in so many innovative ways! Below, we take a closer look at each of the methods noted above.

Pre-recorded worship, weekly sermons, and musical offerings that are filmed in "one take" can be done with a simple smartphone, computer, or basic recording camera. For best results recording with a phone or camera, purchase a simple tripod or stand to provide stability for the camera and allow the leader to focus on the words or music you are offering. The "one-take" option, while not as polished as edited versions, allows for both simplicity and authenticity. Be honest with your congregation that this recording is essentially "live," even though it's pre-recorded. Be honest with yourself that the "one-take" option leaves you more vulnerable as a leader than edited versions. This option frees up an enormous amount of time and cost over methods requiring extensive editing, so that worship isn't the only ministry you have the time or money to provide in a given week. For distribution and communication ideas, see the next paragraph.

Pre-recorded worship filmed in various segments from multiple leaders and locations that are distributed as individual elements allows diverse and varied worship moments to be shared with your fellowship throughout the week, rather than as a single service. One pastor walked his deserted streets the first week communities were sheltering at home as his videographer recorded him with a drone video camera. The voice-over (added later) was both haunting and comforting as the pastor shared both his concerns and his hopes for his congregation and our world. Another pastor recorded all of her summer sermons from her dock, with a beautiful lake in the background, taking her congregation through a series of "lakeshore" stories of Jesus and the disciples. In both cases, their churches also distributed links to instrumental and vocal music from their church musicians. One church included weekly links to children's messages from volunteers in their Christian education program. When individuals use their own equipment to record these segments, the quality can vary widely. Some churches address this issue by having participants visit the sanctuary at scheduled times so that a videographer can record each segment, or they advise participants in use of common equipment and methods. For example, one church asks each volunteer who records a prayer or song to record it horizontally on a smartphone, using the phone's built-in microphone. Some church administrators and pastors share the links to the various recordings on the church website or in emails with PDF documents. Others post each segment on their social media channels as the segment is created, which allows for spiritual nurture throughout the week. Others wait and send all of the links in a weekly post to create a more unified feel to worship, even when it is created in different segments. Consider sharing prayers and readings from this resource with a variety of volunteer and staff worship leaders throughout your worship year, to expand both participation and creativity in the worship experience. Remind them they are permitted to adapt, edit, or use the resources exactly as they are written in both written and recorded format. Just note the authorship and copyright notice in whatever written communication accompanies your recordings.

Pre-recorded worship filmed in various segments from multiple leaders and locations edited into one worship

service provides a fuller and more familiar worship experience for congregants. As with the previous style, recording from various locations provides a great deal of creativity and variety, but varying sound levels and quality of recordings can present a challenge for your video editor. Most churches find that the editing is simplified if all recordings are shot in one location using the same equipment, with leaders scheduled at various times to provide for safe physical distancing. This option requires more preparation and planning, along with a paid editor or very generous volunteer who can handle the demands of post-production editing. Our son, Michael Beu, a video editor, works with a number of churches and pastors to manage the technical and time-consuming demands of editing and posting their worship videos, or helps them find volunteers or train staff members to do so. This extra help allows pastors to focus on worship rather than on technology, and many church donors have stepped up to provide the financial support necessary for this new way of providing worship and spiritual nurture.

For the worship experience, some churches "premiere" worship services put together in this way by scheduling the uploaded video to go "live" at a specific time on their social media channel. This allows and encourages congregants to watch and worship "together" at the same time from their various locations and also can provide viewers the opportunity for interactive chat on the social media channel, creating a sense of community. This sense of community is increased if the worship service is followed by a virtual fellowship time via video conferencing on platforms like Zoom or Skype. Others "open" the posted worship service video immediately, once editing and uploading is complete, so that worshipers can view and worship whenever they want. One of our readers prefers this latter option, so that her church can join for virtual fellowship and sermon conversation during the normal Sunday morning worship time, having viewed worship the day before.

Pre-recorded musical offerings filmed from multiple participants and locations that are edited into a virtual choir or ensemble allow vocal music and ensemble music to be a part of our lives even when it is unsafe to "make music" in the same space or when we want to create ensembles with people who live in different parts of the globe. Solo offerings are, of course, more easily achieved even with simple recording devices—sometimes connected directly to an electronic musical instrument, other times recorded with the internal microphone provided on the recording device. Most musicians prefer the higher quality of recording with an external microphone, attached to the video-recording device. Virtual ensembles require a great deal of post-production sound editing. It's harder than it looks and sounds, and yet many brave musicians and film editors have taken on the task and learned the necessary technology to bring these virtual ensembles to their congregations.

Livestreamed sermons, meditations, or devotionals are being offered by churches at all times of day and night around our globe. They can be recorded and offered on almost any social media channel by clicking on their livestream option. One colleague records a daily devotional video, but also posts it in written format on his Facebook page. (He also enlists church leaders to record on Fridays and Saturdays, so he can enjoy sabbath and family time on those days.) Consider using prayers and responsive readings from this resource to enhance devotionals, sermons, or reflective meditations you are providing for your people.

Livestreamed worship services that include sermons, music, and liturgy require recording equipment connected to a livestreaming service and, ideally, a wired connection to the internet. Most churches who choose this option have invested considerable money into a streaming broadcast system and budget for trained staff members who know how to operate both the recording and broadcasting systems. As with the virtual choir option, this isn't as easy as it looks! But it is a beautiful option for churches that have the ability and the resources. That said, most churches who were streaming before the pandemic have both adapted and improved their livestream worship ministry. Before the pandemic, much of livestreamed worship was either an afterthought of what was already happening on Sundays or a polished "performance." Now, some of the fanciest live streams have become the simplest. There is an elegance to this simplicity and this intentionality, when worship is crafted to focus on one primary theme or message. Worship services have been shortened to adapt to the shorter attention span of a virtual congregation. Messages and musical offerings are less polished and more personal, creating intimacy and relationship with viewers at home. Don't be fooled, though! The technology in the background to make livestreaming successful is complex with little room for error, which occurs frequently for a variety of reasons. Those of us who livestream on a regular basis have learned to laugh at ourselves, forgive technology, and patiently await our technicians to address the glitches that inevitably arise. One colleague laughingly posted on our clergy Facebook group, "It's time to designate a 'Glitch Sunday!'"

Video-conference worship, using providers like Zoom, provides opportunities for interaction and fellowship during the worship experience. While this format creates a more collaborative environment, it requires more flexibility and informality for both leaders and participants. Best practice for this format has participants and members log onto the video conference *with a private church link* in order to prevent interruptions by internet trolls. Designate a video-conference coordinator to welcome guests, help with password and technology challenges, monitor chat questions or comments, and mute everyone but the participants once worship begins. A video-conference coordinator allows pastors, musicians, and worship leaders to focus on their worship responsibilities without having to control the service's complicated technical requirements.

When the pastor and designated leaders are leading, their video feeds should be the only ones with active microphones. This allows people to hear more clearly and participate more fully without interrupting the worship flow. While microphones are muted, congregational singing, unison and responsive readings, and responses to the Spirit are all possible in this format. If you have a solo worship leader, make sure their microphone is always unmuted so that they can lead the singing, readings, and prayers. To add an interactive component, encourage people to comment in their chat box, or even invite conversation following the message by designating a time of unmuted sermon feedback and Q & A. Similarly, community prayer, and joys and concerns can be interactive by unmuting members for these worship elements; but be sure to mute the members again before praying the pastoral or the Lord's Prayer. Although you can use a webinar format instead, webinars are more "presentation" than "participation," similar to a Facebook Live or YouTube Premiere.

Choosing or Changing Your Version of Virtual Worship

Several decisions need to be made before settling on a method of virtual worship:

> 1. Whom is God calling your church to reach? What technology are they able and willing to access?

2. What type of worship experience will best serve the congregation you are called to reach?

3. How much is your church able and willing to spend, both in time and money?

4. What technology and distribution platform best addresses these questions?

With these decisions in mind, you are ready to work with your worship team to create a virtual worship design and choose a platform best suited to your current needs. What you started with need not limit where you go in 2023 and beyond. Similarly, if you've been doing this alone, you need not continue doing it alone. This is the perfect time to create a worship team that will work with you, supporting and strengthening both the process and creativity of your worship experience. When planned and implemented alone, virtual worship is already leading to many early retirements and departures from ministry. The workload is simply too exhausting and isolating to sustain by one individual, regardless of how talented they are. Reach out to your leadership, your colleagues, and even community partners to find the help you need. If you're reading this article but not on the worship team, check with your pastor or musician to see if they need support and help. Contact us if you need help figuring out how to find and work with a team.

Adapting Music and Liturgy for Social Distancing and Safety

One of the greatest challenges in church worship today has been the limitations placed on vocal music and the spoken word to avoid spreading infection. Yet, limitations give rise to creativity and new ways for musicians to stay involved in ministry. Some vocal choirs have transitioned into bell choirs. Other vocalists have been reading the texts of favorite hymns or anthems, while instrumentalists play the music underneath. Some churches are pre-recording vocal music for presentation on-screen during live worship, while simultaneously streaming the live worship and the pre-recorded music for their virtual worshipers. Responsive and unison readings are not always the safest option for a congregation gathered together, but two readers may "duet" a responsive reading from the chancel while remaining safely distanced from both worshipers and one another. Or again, music might enhance a solo voice reciting the Lord's Prayer. Looking for more creative ideas? Visit **maryscifresministries.com** to find some of the creative ways B. J. and Mary are working to address the changing forms of worship.

Adapting Virtual Worship to a Hybrid Form

Over these last few years, you have likely led worship in a variety of ways, adapting to social restrictions the pandemic has thrown our way. As churches re-open their sanctuaries, while also offering virtual worship, we have begun calling this new *both-and* situation *hybrid worship*. Our worship services are no longer just the old fossil-fueled combustion engine of sanctuary worship, but also electric-fueled worship of videos streamed directly into the homes of church members and friends around the globe. One colleague welcomed a North Carolina family into membership in his California church three thousand miles away. When their sanctuary reopened, the North Carolina family continued to participate and connect through the many online worship and study group opportunities of their California church home, growing more and more deeply connected regardless of geographical distance. As congregations again gather for in-person worship, this hybrid model allows us to continue serving our virtual worshipers. To prepare for this, worship leaders have put tech crews in place who can record the services, upload to an online platform, and communicate with the congregation how to access the online service. Your best practice is for worship leaders to focus on the worship components (music, message, liturgy) and for tech and administrative team members to focus on the technology and communication components. Let us know if you have questions or concerns we can help you address, or if you have insights and ideas to share with others.

Mary Scifres & B. J. Beu
admin@maryscifres.com

January 1, 2024

New Year's Day

Anna Crews Camphouse

COLOR

White

SCRIPTURE READINGS

Ecclesiastes 3:1-13; Psalm 8; Revelation 21:1-6a;
Matthew 25:31-46

THEME IDEAS

Following the way of Christ can feel overwhelming and
daunting. However, God's goodness and abundance are
resurrecting and restorative for all of creation, including
us. Recommitting ourselves to the Christian walk this
New Year's Day requires praise of God's faithfulness,
trust in God's mercy, and a willingness to open ourselves up to God's provision. Only then can we be the
vessels of hope God calls us to be.

INVITATION AND GATHERING

CENTERING PRAYER (*Ecclesiastes 3*)
For all the blessings of seasons past,
    we give you thanks, O God.

For all the wonders of seasons yet to come,
we give you praise.

CALL TO WORSHIP (Psalm 8)

Everything that lives is imbued with the spark
of God's divine creativity.
How majestic is God's name in all the earth!
The sovereign Spirit of life breathes hope into us
to fulfill new possibilities, dreams, and visions.
How majestic is God's name in all the earth!
The creator of all empowers us with a love so strong
it can silence the voices of fear and vengeance.
How majestic is God's name in all the earth!
May God shine through us like stars of promise,
crowning us with the glory of your light.
How majestic is God's name in all the earth!

OPENING PRAYER (Ecclesiastes 3)

Keeper of time, we come to this moment,
remembering the past and envisioning the future.
We know that all things are held tenderly in your care.
Your will for us is a deep and abiding joy,
as we live each day with passion and purpose.
Show us again the path of holy toil,
that we may find meaning and peace
in the work you lay before us.
Seasons change, but your call remains steadfast.
We come today, yearning to hear your voice anew.
Amen.

PROCLAMATION AND RESPONSE

PRAYER OF YEARNING (Revelation 21)

Lover of our souls, when we see only our faults
or the broken pieces of our lives,
you see us as beloved children.

2

Fill the scars of our hearts
    with the gold of deep healing,
        and strengthen our compassion
            with empathy for the hurts of others.
Dwell with us in our innermost thoughts,
    transforming them from despair to gratitude.
Wipe the tears from our eyes,
    and make us buoyant with joy.
We pray these things in the name of our healing savior,
    Jesus, the Christ. Amen.

WORDS OF ASSURANCE (*Revelation 21*)
See, God is making all things new!
It is done. The Alpha and Omega makes it so!

PASSING THE PEACE OF CHRIST (*Matthew 25*)
There are no strangers here, only the face of God in many forms. Let us greet one another with joy, knowing that God embraces us through the love we find in this place. Let us meet one another with compassion and grace, channeling divine abundance and acknowledging our need.

RESPONSE TO THE WORD (*Matthew 25*)
In a sea of faces filled with need,
    demands pull us down like an undertow,
        draining our energy and sapping our strength.
You are the creator of the oceans and of each soul.
You give us the power to swim, float,
    even walk on water.
You give us all we require to do our part.
We come before you not sure we are ready,
    but we are willing still.
Show us how to navigate these waters.
Calm our souls, strengthen our resolve,
    and empower us for a new year of service. Amen.

THANKSGIVING AND COMMUNION

OFFERING PRAYER (Matthew 25)
You ask much of us, O God:
>meals for the hungry
>>and water for those who thirst.
You ask us to give from our abundance:
>clothes for the naked
>>and care for the sick.
You demand mercy and kindness:
>compassion for strangers
>>and generosity to the downtrodden
>>and imprisoned.
We offer these things as well as our gifts
>of time, talent, and resources.
Accept these offerings and bless them to your service.
Lead us, Great Shepherd,
>to the people who need you most. Amen.

INVITATION TO COMMUNION
Whether we have all things or nothing,
>God meets us where we are.
We are not our circumstances.
We are not our labels.
We are individual lights of divine inspiration,
>seeking to join our hearts with our Source,
>>that we may live as Christ.
Come to this moment with your whole selves,
>that God may nurture the divine spark within you.

COMMUNION PRAYER
Giver of Life, years come and go,
>but your love remains eternal.
We bring our broken hearts, wildest dreams,
>inner struggles, deepest needs, confusion, certainty,
>>and we place them at the table of your wisdom.

We come seeking the wine of resurrecting hope
    and the bread of purpose and commitment.
Restore us, renew us, and ready us
    for the tasks, blessings, and adventure
        of the year ahead.
In the name of Christ Jesus, the one who calls us
    and equips us to serve, we pray. Amen.

GREAT THANKSGIVING

The Lord be with you.
    And also with you.
Lift up your hearts.
    We lift them up to the Lord.
Let us give thanks to the Lord our God.
    It is right to give our thanks and praise.

It is right, and a good and joyful thing,
    always and everywhere to give thanks to you:
    in seasons of hopefulness and joy,
    in seasons of sadness and longing,
    in seasons of plenty,
    in seasons of want,
    in seasons when we are ready and willing,
    in seasons when we struggle to simply breathe,
    in seasons when we are loved by many,
    in seasons when we are so lonely it hurts.

For being always with us, we praise your name,
    joining the unending hymn of the faithful on earth
    and all the company of heaven:
    Holy, Holy, Holy Lord, God of power and might;
        heaven and earth are full of your glory.
    Hosanna in the highest. Blessed is the one
        who comes in the name of the Lord.
    Hosanna in the highest.

5

Holy are you and blessed is your Son, Jesus,
    who has shown us the way to salvation.
In feeding the hungry, visiting the imprisoned,
    caring for the sick, and blessing the stranger,
    we see the way to build your commonwealth.
Remind us that your love was made manifest
    when we were hungry, scared, sick, or alone.
Give us empathetic hearts, thoughtful minds,
    and serving spirits.
May we fully embrace the path of our savior
    with a love like his.
We remember that through the baptism
    of his suffering, death, and resurrection,
    you gave birth to your Church,
    delivered us from slavery to sin and death,
    and made with us a new covenant
    by water and the Spirit.

(Words of Institution and Blessing of the Elements)

PRAYER OF CONSECRATION

As we enter into a new year of Christian discipleship,
    unify this body of faithful persons,
        that we may recommit to the service of others
            and to the healing of the communities
                we call home.
Infuse us with your Spirit,
    that we may give praise in all circumstances,
        and find blessings in the midst of challenge.
Bless us with an indomitable hope—
    a hope that transforms even our darkest despair.
Amen.

SENDING FORTH

BENEDICTION (*Ecclesiastes 3, Matthew 25*)
May the shepherding spirit of Christ
    be with you in this new season,
    strengthening you as you strengthen others.
Remembering when you were strangers, sick,
    imprisoned, or in need,
    may you abundantly offer provision for others
    with gratitude and mercy.
Trusting in the never-ending goodness of the Divine,
    may you be a vessel of light and hope
    to our hurting world. Amen.

January 6, 2024

Epiphany of the Lord

Mary Scifres
Copyright © Mary Scifres

COLOR

White

SCRIPTURE READINGS

Isaiah 60:1-6; Psalm 72:1-7, 10-14; Ephesians 3:1-12;
Matthew 2:1-12

THEME IDEAS

The magnetic attraction of light permeates the Epiphany
readings, as does the call to humbly worship Christ, our
King. Light draws the wise men from the East to Jerusalem, echoing Isaiah's prophetic promise that nations will
come to the dawning of God's glorious light. Similarly,
light draws our attention: in the shorter days of winter,
on a sparkling Christmas tree, or a festively decorated
home. Light attracts us, as surely as it draws moths to a
flame. Christ, the Light of the World, calls to our hearts
in the same way. But today's readings invite us to approach the light humbly, adoring the glory and bowing
in worship before the Christ child.

INVITATION AND GATHERING

CENTERING WORDS *(Isaiah 60, Psalm 72, John 8:12)*
As we focus on the Light of the World, God's vision of justice and love grows clearer and shines more brightly in our thoughts and actions.

CALL TO WORSHIP *(Isaiah 60, Matthew 2)*
Christ's light is shining,
calling us to respond with joy.
Christ's light is shining,
calling us to worship and praise.

OPENING PRAYER *(Isaiah 60, Psalm 72)*
God of glory and grace, shine upon our worship
with your presence.
Shine in our hearts with your love.
Shine in our lives with your grace,
that we may arise with confidence
and go forth to bring your justice and love to all.
Amen.

PROCLAMATION AND RESPONSE

PRAYER OF CONFESSION *(Isaiah 60, Ephesians 3, Matthew 5)*
Merciful God, grant us the grace to behold your glory
and offer us the assurance that your loving light
will not burn us.
Grant us the confidence
that we too can shine your light in our world.
Remove the lampshades of fear and shame
that hide our light.

Dust off the cobwebs of doubt and despair
>   that shadow our light.
Shine in and through us,
>   that your light may brighten our world. Amen.

WORDS OF ASSURANCE *(Ephesians 3, John 8, Matthew 5)*
Here is the mystery: Grace is ours, no matter what.
God's love is ours, no matter what.
Grace and love save us and shine in us.
They allow us to shine as the light of the world
>   with the Light of the World. Amen.

PASSING THE PEACE OF CHRIST *(Psalm 72)*
May we be like rain that falls on the mown grass, nourishing and renewing one another with God's peace and love. May we share signs of this peace and love with notes of kindness, symbols of love, and actions of justice.
(Encourage online worshipers to share comments of peace and joy on your video platform. If appropriate, invite all worshipers to take a moment to send a text message of joy and love to someone who isn't in worship today.)

INTRODUCTION TO THE WORD *(Ephesians 3, Psalm 19)*
May God's wisdom shine through the words of our mouths, the thoughts of our minds, and the meditations of our hearts.

RESPONSIVE PRAYER IN RESPONSE TO THE WORD
(Psalm 72)
Give us justice, O God.
>   **that we may be justice-bringers to your world.**
Give us righteousness, O God,
>   **that we may live righteousness**
>   **in love and compassion.**

Give us light, O God,
    that we bring light to the shadows
    and hope to the hopeless.
Give us peace, O God,
    that we may be peacemakers in all that we do
    and in all that we say. Amen.

THANKSGIVING AND COMMUNION

INVITATION TO THE OFFERING (Isaiah 60, Matthew 2)
As we gaze on the lights of the Christmas season,
    may we remember the Light that draws near.
Like those wise travelers from the East,
    let us bring gifts and treasurers to honor Christ,
    the Light of the World.

OFFERING PRAYER (Isaiah 60, Matthew 2)
Glorious God, bring glory to these gifts
    and to the offering we share
        with you and your church.
Bring the light of your justice and righteousness
    to the dark corners of our world.
Bring the glory of your love and compassion
    to heal our broken communities.
Bring the hope of generosity and gratitude
    to places in need of transformation. Amen.

INVITATION TO COMMUNION (Matthew 2)
Follow the star to the table of grace.
    Here we find gifts beyond price.
Follow the star to the table of blessing.
    Here we find strength for the journey.
Follow the star to the table of peace.
    Here we find rest and refreshment.
Follow the star to the table of Christ.
    Here we find light and love.

THE GREAT THANKSGIVING[1] *(Isaiah 60, Psalm 72, Ephesians 3, Matthew 2)*
The Lord be with you.
> **And also with you.**

Lift up your hearts.
> **We lift them up to the Lord.**

Let us give thanks to the Lord, our God.
> **It is right to give our thanks and praise.**

It is right, and a good and joyful thing,
> always and everywhere to give thanks to you,
> Almighty God, creator of heaven and earth.

In ancient days, you created us in your image
> to shine like the sun as reflections of your glory.

When we hid from your glory,
> and the brilliance of your light within us dimmed,
> you led us out of the garden
> and into the four corners of the earth.

From ancient times, through all the ages,
> you have saved us from the forces of darkness,
> and have guided us with the light of your love.

From the bondage of slavery,
> you led us out of Egypt with a pillar of fire,
> and even now, your holy fire of love leads us still.

And so, with your people on earth,
> and all the company of heaven,
> we praise your name and join their unending hymn:
> **Holy, holy, holy Lord, God of power and might,**
> > **heaven and earth are full of your glory.**
> **Hosanna in the highest. Blessed is the one**
> > **who comes in the name of the Lord.**
> **Hosanna in the highest.**

Holy are you and blessed is the Light of the World,
> Christ Jesus, whom kings from the Orient worshiped
> after following his natal star to a household of love.

Jesus shone with a light too wonderful
    for the forces of darkness to endure.
His ministry and teachings stand, even today,
    as beacons of justice and righteousness
    in a world darkened by oppression and hate.
Through Jesus' humble beginnings,
    you invite us to live simply,
    that others may simply live.
Through Christ's patient love and unfailing grace,
    your light shines on us with forgiveness
    and your grace blesses us with deliverance,
    that as your redeemed children,
    we might shine your light in the world
    as signs of hope and love.
On the night when Jesus faced the darkness,
    he offered signs of light as he took the bread,
    gave thanks to you, broke the bread,
    and gave it to his disciples, saying:
    "Take, eat; this is my body which is given for you.
    Do this in remembrance of me."
When the supper was over
    and Jesus prepared to face his darkest fears,
    he took the cup, gave thanks to you,
    and gave it to his disciples,
    even those who would betray and reject him, saying:
    "Drink from this, all of you;
    this is my life poured out for you and for many
    for the forgiveness of sins.
    Do this, as often as you drink it,
    in remembrance of me."

With joy and gratitude, we break this bread,
    remembering the many times Jesus was revealed
    to his disciples in the breaking of the bread.

In remembrance, we will take and eat this bread.
With faith and hope, we take this cup,
> remembering Jesus' gifts of grace and forgiveness,
> poured out for his disciples of yesterday,
> today, and tomorrow.
In remembrance, we will take and drink of this cup.

And so, in remembrance of your mighty acts,
> and your signs of light and life in Jesus Christ,
> we offer ourselves in praise and thanksgiving,
> as signs of light and life,
> in union with Christ's offering for us,
> as we proclaim the mystery of faith:
> **Christ has died.**
> **Christ is risen.**
> **Christ will come again.**

PRAYER OF CONSECRATION (Isaiah 60:1-6, Psalm 72)

Pour out your Holy Spirit on us,
> that we may be your light in the world.
Pour out your Holy Spirit
> on these gifts of bread and wine,
>> that we may be filled with your glory and grace.
By your Spirit, make us one with Christ,
> one with one another,
>> and one in ministry to all the world,
>>> until Christ comes in final victory
>>>> and we feast at your heavenly banquet.
Through your Son, Jesus Christ,
> with the Holy Spirit in your holy Church,
>> all honor and glory is yours, Almighty God,
>>> now and forevermore. Amen.

GIVING THE BREAD AND CUP
(The bread and wine are given to the people with these or other words of blessing.)
The light of Christ, shining through you.
The glory of God, blazing within you.

SENDING FORTH

BENEDICTION (Isaiah 60, Psalm 72)
Go forth to shine with light of Christ's love.
Go forth to shine with the glory of Christ's grace.
Go forth to shine with the justice and peace
of Christ's life.

1. Beu, B. J. and Scifres, Mary. Excerpted from *Is It Communion Sunday Already?! Communion Resources for All Seasons.* © 2017 B. J. Beu and Mary Scifres. Used by permission of the authors. Full resource available for purchase on Amazon.

January 7, 2024

Baptism of the Lord

Mary Petrina Boyd

COLOR

White

SCRIPTURE READINGS

Genesis 1:1-5; Psalm 29; Acts 19:1-7; Mark 1:4-11

THEME IDEAS

We hear God's word in many ways. In Genesis 1, God speaks and creation begins. Psalm 29 describes God's voice as a mighty wind. As Jesus rises from the waters of the river Jordan, he hears God speak words of blessing. At the start of a new calendar year, we begin anew. As we celebrate the baptism of the Lord, we celebrate new beginnings, for God is always at work, creating and calling forth blessings.

INVITATION AND GATHERING

CENTERING WORDS (Mark 1)
You are God's beloved child. God is pleased with you.

CALL TO WORSHIP (Genesis 1)
> In the beginning . . .
>> **God.**
> In the beginning . . .
>> **God's Spirit.**
> In the beginning . . .
>> **God's Word.**
> In the beginning . . .
>> **God's Light.**
> In the beginning . . .
>> **a new day.**
> A new beginning for every day.
>> **God's gift of creation.**

–OR–

CALL TO WORSHIP (Genesis 1, Psalm 29, Mark 1)
> Listen for God's word . . .
>> **calling forth creation.**
> Listen for God's word . . .
>> **working with power and majesty.**
> Listen for God's word . . .
>> **speaking blessings.**
> Listen for God's word . . .
>> **in this moment.**

OPENING PRAYER (Genesis 1, Psalm 29)
> God of power and majesty, you call forth creation,
>> acting with strength and power.
> We praise you, as we stand in awe of your glory.
> You are mighty and powerful, and yet you care for us,
>> pouring your Spirit of love upon us,
>> recreating us for your work in the world.
> You are at work in our midst,
>> offering a new day of hope and possibility.
> Open our hearts to the sound of your voice.

Send the power of your Spirit among us,
   that we might become agents
      of your love and peace. Amen.

PROCLAMATION AND RESPONSE

PRAYER OF YEARNING *(Genesis 1, Mark 1)*
God, we are so tired.
The holidays were a wonderful, busy time,
   as we celebrated the birth of Jesus.
As we return to life without festive celebrations,
   we long to avoid feeling let down or discouraged.
Teach us to listen for your gentle voice.
Help us awaken to the quiet stirrings of new life
   in our hearts and in our communities.
As your children, called into being by your word,
   remake and renew us,
      that we may follow you with joy. Amen.

WORDS OF ASSURANCE *(Mark 1)*
You are God's child, God's beloved creation.
Receive God's offer of new life and new beginnings.

PASSING THE PEACE OF CHRIST *(Mark 1)*
You are members of God's beloved community. Greet
one another with the peace of Christ.

RESPONSE TO THE WORD *(Mark 1, Acts 19)*
God of wonder and majesty, we hear your voice
   calling us to follow your Son, your beloved.
Baptized into Jesus, you also call us your beloved.
When we are afraid, when we doubt our own worth,
   we hear your voice reaching out to us,
      declaring our value,
         affirming your love for us.

18

Give us faith to set aside our doubts and fears,
    that we may live courageously,
        knowing that you love us. Amen.

THANKSGIVING AND COMMUNION

INVITATION TO THE OFFERING *(Genesis 1, Psalm 29)*
Over and over, God's creating Spirit
    blows through our lives.
In our giving, we respond to this Spirit.

OFFERING PRAYER *(Genesis 1)*
God of strength and glory, you created all that is.
You continue to sustain the world
    with the power of your love.
You give us life and hope,
    and with grateful hearts, we bring these gifts to you.
May they bring forth your realm of peace
    for all peoples. Amen.

GREAT THANKSGIVING *(Genesis 1, Psalm 29)*
God of beginnings, you are always creating.
At the very beginning, you sent your Spirit
    to bring order out of chaos.
You spoke and there was light.
You named the light day,
    and the darkness you called light.
It was the first morning, a new beginning.
You continued your active presence in our world,
    over and over calling forth newness.
With power and might,
    you spoke through the wind and storm,
    washing away past sorrow
    as you cleaned the world and began anew.

When we followed our own desires,
    ignoring the promises of your word,
    you sent prophets to speak of life and peace.
You never gave up on us,
    but kept on reaching out to us
    through the power of your Spirit.

And so, we join the great chorus of heaven and earth,
praising you forever.
    Holy, holy, holy, God of glory and strength!
    Holy, holy, holy, God of power and majesty!
    Heaven and earth are filled with your splendor.
    Hosanna in the highest.
    Blessed is Jesus, who comes in your name.
    Hosanna in the highest.

You spoke through the prophet, John the baptizer.
In the wilderness, John spoke your word,
    calling people to repentance
    and declaring that one who is more powerful
    is coming.
That one was Jesus. And as he emerged
    from the waters of the Jordan, you proclaimed,
    "You are my son, the Beloved.
    With you I am well pleased."
Jesus continued to live as your word in the world.
He built a community of God's beloved persons,
    welcoming everyone.
He offered a word of hope and encouragement
    to the discouraged.
He challenged the powerful to work for justice.
In the life and ministry of Jesus,
    there was a new beginning for creation.

As Jesus faced condemnation and death,
    he gathered his friends for a meal.
He took bread, gave thanks to you, broke it,
    and gave it to his friends, saying:
        "This is my life, offered for you.
        When you eat this, remember me."
When the meal was over, he took the cup,
    gave thanks to you
    and offered it to his friends, saying:
        "This is the cup of forgiveness,
        poured out in abundance.
        When you drink it, remember me."

And so, as we remember Jesus
    and his ministry of love and forgiveness,
    we proclaim the mystery of faith:
    Christ was. Christ is. Christ will be.

It looked like the end of Jesus ministry,
    yet he offered a new beginning with this meal—
    a meal that binds us together as a holy,
    beloved community.

God of glory, send your Spirit upon these gifts
    of bread and cup.
May they become a new beginning for our lives,
    by feeding us for your work in the world.
Send your Spirit upon us, gathered at this table.
May we become the living body of Christ,
    expressing your love in word and deed.
Through your child Jesus,
    and by the power of your Holy Spirit in your Church,
        all glory and strength, power and majesty
            are yours, now and forevermore.
    Amen.

21

SENDING FORTH

BENEDICTION (*Genesis 1, Psalm 29, Mark 1*)
> May the God of love strengthen you
> to serve creation with joy.
> May God bless you with deep peace.
> Named as God's beloved, go forth,
> building new communities of blessing for others.

January 14, 2024

Second Sunday after the Epiphany

B. J. Beu
Copyright © B. J. Beu

COLOR

Green

SCRIPTURE READINGS

1 Samuel 3:1-10, (11-20); Psalm 139:1-6, 13-18;
1 Corinthians 6:12-20; John 1:43-51

THEME IDEAS

God calls us when we are young, when we are middle-aged, even when the sun is setting in our lives. Because of this, much is expected of us. If we pay attention and open our eyes, we will truly see God's wondrous works in our lives. The psalmist marvels at being fearfully and wonderfully made. Paul warns us that our bodies are temples of the Holy Spirit and that we should therefore glorify God in how we treat our bodies. Finally, Nathaniel is convinced to follow Jesus because Jesus "saw him" sitting under a fig tree. Whether we are lying down or merely growing in our mother's wombs, God searches us and knows us, comes to us and ministers to us, and is with us and within us. With such indwelling of body and Spirit, how can we fail to respond to God's call like Samuel: "Speak, LORD, for your servant is listening" (v. 9).

INVITATION AND GATHERING

CENTERING WORDS (Psalm 139)
Let all who draw breath shout for joy and sing praises to the living God.

CALL TO WORSHIP (1 Samuel 3, Psalm 139, John 1)
Speak to us, Lord, for your servants are listening.
The One who fashioned us in our mother's womb calls us this day.
Lead us, O God, and we will follow.
The One acquainted with all our ways leads us into life.
Bless us, Spirit of wisdom and truth, and guide us home.
The One who hems us in, from behind and before, is a lamp to our feet.
Speak to us, Lord, for your servants are listening.

OPENING PRAYER (1 Samuel 3, Psalm 139, John 1)
Before you formed us in our mother's womb,
  you knew us completely.
Before a word is on our lips,
  you perceive it.
You hem us in, before and behind.
You call us as your own
  and lay your hand upon us.
Such knowledge is too wonderful for us;
  it is so high we cannot attain it.
Even when we fail, Holy One, call us anew,
  that we might hear your voice
    and respond with expectation and joy:
      "Here I am." Amen.

PROCLAMATION AND RESPONSE

PRAYER OF YEARNING (1 Samuel 3, Psalm 139, John 1)
God of a thousand voices, we yearn to hear your call:
when we lie down to sleep,
when we rise to meet the sun,
when we offer our industry,
when we gather with family and friends.
Speak to us once more, Lord of life,
when we mistake your call
or dismiss it as a dream.
Hem us in with your power and your might,
that we may feel your hand leading us
and your love guiding our way,
through Christ Jesus, our Lord. Amen.

WORDS OF ASSURANCE (1 Corinthians 6, John 1)
God never gives up on us, and Christ never forsakes us.
Rejoice and be glad, for we are one in the Spirit;
we are one in the Lord.

PASSING THE PEACE OF CHRIST (John 1)
Just as infants find comfort being swaddled in a blanket, may we find the peace of Christ as God hems us in, behind and before, with holy love. Let us share signs of this peace with one another today.

INTRODUCTION TO THE WORD (1 Samuel 3)
Listen, the voice of God is calling.
Speak, Lord, for your servants are listening.

RESPONSE TO THE WORD (1 Samuel 3, Psalm 139,
1 Corinthians 6, John 1)
> God calls us this day:
>> **by touching our minds with wisdom and truth,**
>> **by healing our hearts with love and joy,**
>> **by blessing our bodies with vitality and strength,**
>> **by reviving our souls with fullness of grace.**
> With every fiber of your being, offer your reply:
>> **"Here I am, for you called me."**

THANKSGIVING AND COMMUNION

INVITATION TO THE OFFERING (John 1)
> Can anything good come out of a Nazareth? Come and
> see. Can this church be the body of Christ? Come and
> see. Can our gifts make a difference in the world? Come
> and see. Let us give generously this morning, that the
> whole world may come and see the blessings of God.

OFFERING PRAYER (1 Samuel 3, Psalm 139,
1 Corinthians 6, John 1)
> God of vision and courage,
>> you call us to be your hands and feet in the world.
> In a world full of need,
>> use our gifts and our offerings,
>>> our time and our talents,
>>>> to bless those in need of your blessings.
> Through these gifts,
>> may others come to see your grace
>>> and hear your call in their lives. Amen.

SENDING FORTH

BENEDICTION (1 Samuel 3, John 1)
Wherever you go, speak words of love and grace
to everyone you meet.
**We will speak words of hope and faith
to gladden the heart and strengthen the spirit.**
As those who are called by the living God,
invite others to hear Christ's call in their lives.
**We will remind all God's children
that God is speaking still.**

January 21, 2024

Third Sunday after the Epiphany

Leigh Ann Shaw

COLOR

Green

SCRIPTURE READINGS

Jonah 3:1-5, 10; Psalm 62:5-12; 1 Corinthians 7:29-31;
Mark 1:14-20

THEME IDEAS

The season of Epiphany slowly moves from the darkness of waiting to the expansive light of awareness.
These scriptures tell the story of our call from God and
our discipleship journey. God's call informs the readings from both Jonah and Mark. All the scriptures taken
together reflect human distraction and willfulness and
the need to be grounded in God. The psalmist yokes our
divided, distracted hearts and spirits with the balm of
silence and the blessing of assurance.

INVITATION AND GATHERING

CENTERING WORDS (Psalm 62)
God is not a taskmaster keeping track of our good deeds.
Rather, God intervenes boldly and relentlessly for the
purpose of life and the restoration of creation.

CALL TO WORSHIP (Psalm 62, Jonah 3, Mark 1)
Gathered in worship with silence and sound,
we wait upon God's grace.
Gathered in worship with focused heart and mind,
we anticipate the time we face.

**OPENING PRAYER or PRAYER OF CONFESSION
(Psalm 62, Jonah 3, Mark 1)**
God of unifying grace,
we come distracted by the world.
Our minds wander,
and are filled with thoughts other than you.
Our hearts are confused,
and we are uncertain where we belong.
Call us to follow you once more.
Redeem the night and bless the day
that greets us this morning.
May your relentless ways never fail
as we strive to live as your beloved people.
Amen.

PROCLAMATION AND RESPONSE

PRAYER OF CONFESSION (Jonah 3, Mark 1)
Holy One, you have called us from the seashore
to service in this world.
You have pulled us from our comfort
to embrace the inconvenience of servanthood.
You have put before us an opportunity
that we never truly wanted.
Like Jonah, who resented going where you sent him,
we are restless and resistant.
We'd rather sleep in a boat
and go about a casual kind of life.

> We'd rather live our days as we always have
>> and let the tides carry us where they will.
> May the storms of our days shake us
>> to new awareness and renewed paths
>>> of faithful living. Amen.

WORDS OF ASSURANCE (Jonah 3, Mark 1)

Hear the good news!
Before you turned to God, God was on watch for you.
Before you remembered your sin,
God extended redeeming grace.
Hear these words: You are forgiven.
**Thanks be that God stands watch
over our very lives.
Thanks be to God for the grace
that meets us where we are.
Hear these words: You are forgiven.**

PASSING THE PEACE OF CHRIST (Mark 1)

Jesus comes to us, proclaiming the good news. He challenges us to acknowledge our wandering heart and to remember that we are loved. As children, forgiven by grace, let us take time now to extend peace to one another.

INTRODUCTION TO THE WORD (Jonah 3 and Mark 1)

The Word of God meets us where we are. God's call came to Jonah and found resistance. But even as an unwilling prophet, Jonah relented and brought judgment to the people of Nineveh. God's call came to fishermen on a seashore. Unlike Jonah, these men responded faithfully and immediately. As we listen to these scriptures, rather than judging how others respond to their call, consider how we respond to God's call in our lives. God is always leading humanity toward redemption and forgiveness, even when hearts are resistant.

RESPONSE TO THE WORD (Jonah 3 and Mark 1)
God's word is shared to open our eyes
and quicken our spirits.
Thanks be to God.

THANKSGIVING AND COMMUNION

INVITATION TO THE OFFERING (Psalm 62)
This is our time of offering, where we respond with gratitude to all that God has given us. Let us take a moment to consider what gifts we will bring and what commitments to action we will make this week.

OFFERING PRAYER (Mark 1)
Restorer of divided hearts,
bless our gifts this morning.
Make our offering a path to holy living and action.
May our very lives reflect the truth of our faith
and our commitment to your world.
With generous hearts, we pray. Amen.

SENDING FORTH

BENEDICTION (Jonah 3, Mark 1)
The kingdom of God is near.
We are called to action.
The kingdom of God unfolds throughout our lives.
We will take the word of grace into the world.
Go, redeemed and blessed, for you are never alone.
We will spread the good news! Amen.

January 28, 2024

Fourth Sunday after the Epiphany

Rebecca Gaudino

COLOR

Green

SCRIPTURE READINGS

Deuteronomy 18:15-20; Psalm 111; 1 Corinthians 8:1-13; Mark 1:21-28

THEME IDEAS

Our Gospel account takes place shortly after Jesus' baptism, when the Spirit descends on Jesus and declares him to be: "my Son, the Beloved" (Mark 1:11, NRSVUE). But now we have a different spirit, one that renders a son of God less than he is intended to be, one that controls, convulses, and uses the man to shout loudly in a place of worship. This spirit is unclean. It is not the Spirit of the cleansing waters of baptism; and rather than being concerned about the well-being of the man it inhabits, this spirit is concerned only for itself: "Have you come to destroy us?" (1:24). The preceding question, however, is amazing for what it comes to mean for the suffering man: "What have you to do with us, Jesus of Nazareth?" (1:24). Jesus has everything to do with this man, who somehow found his way to the synagogue and to the very presence of the Spirit-accompanied Jesus. And he now has the gift of freedom, perhaps even the first experience of silence he has had in a long time. What have you to do with us, Jesus? Everything.

INVITATION AND GATHERING

CENTERING WORDS (Psalm 111, Mark 1)

What have you to do with me, Jesus of Nazareth? What have you to do with my joys and my hopes, with my hurts and my losses? Come with grace and mercy.

CALL TO WORSHIP (Psalm 111, Mark 1)

Fount of Life, Glorious One,
your great works are full of honor and majesty:
> **the earth that we stand on,**
> **the trees that shade us,**
> **the birds that soar above us.**

Ever-Living God, Generous One,
your goodness and faithfulness endure forever:
> **the wisdom we learn,**
> **the justice we long and work for,**
> **the hope you offer.**

Sheltering God, Healing One,
you remember your covenant and its promises to us:
> **the grace and mercy you give,**
> **the healing you offer,**
> **the tenderness you show to us.**

The works of your hands are faithful and just.
Your teachings are trustworthy and true.
> **Your praise endures forever! Amen.**

OPENING PRAYER (Psalm 111)

Faithful God, we stand in this congregation
    to give you thanks with our whole hearts,
        for your works are great.
Your massive power upholds the universe,
    and yet it is so intimate, it upholds our lives,
        tiny in the scale of the galaxies.
You provide food for us and for all your creatures,
    from goldfish to whales,
    hummingbirds to eagles,
    ants to elephants.
You nurture life in the seas,
    yet watch over the deserts.
Your work is full of honor and majesty.
Thank you for being mindful of us all,
    remembering your promises.
May your creative love and faithful power
    endure forever. Amen.

PROCLAMATION AND RESPONSE

PRAYER OF YEARNING (Psalm 111, Mark 1)

Gracious God, when we speak of your great power,
    the power that abounds in creation all around us,
        we sometimes wonder if it is in our own lives.
We hear that you are faithful,
    that you remember us and your promises,
        yet there are places in our lives
            that don't feel quite right.
We often wonder what you have to do with our lives,
    especially in the places that hurt.
Help us trust your promised grace,
    for we long to touch your healing peace. Amen.

WORDS OF ASSURANCE (Psalm 111)
    God holds true to God's promises
        and sends redemption to God's people.
    Let us rejoice in the God who remembers and redeems.
    Amen.

PASSING THE PEACE OF CHRIST (Psalm 111)
    We stand in good company, the congregation of our God
    of righteousness and mercy. Let us greet our siblings in
    the name of our good God.

RESPONSE TO THE WORD (Psalm 111, Mark 1)
    Fount of wisdom and life, Holy One of God,
        your teachings are trustworthy and true.
    They are the beginning of wisdom in our lives.
    May they also be the beginning of peace and hope
        in our world.
    May the divine commands that lit the sky with light,
        be the commands that light our lives
            with your healing power.
    What have you to do with us, Jesus of Nazareth?
    Everything.
    Grant your healing power
        in the hurting and hopeful places of our lives.
    Amen.

THANKSGIVING AND COMMUNION

INVITATION TO THE OFFERING (Psalm 111)
    Let us give thanks for the wonderful deeds of God,
    through our own generosity and faithfulness to others.

OFFERING PRAYER (Psalm 111, Mark 1)
Holy One, Jesus of Nazareth, Spirit from on high,
may our gifts reveal your grace and mercy
far and wide.
May others learn of your faithful love
through the power of your works
and through the gifts we bring this day.
May they also learn
that you have everything to do with their lives.
Amen.

SENDING FORTH

BENEDICTION (Psalm 111, Mark 1)
What have you to do with us, Jesus of Nazareth?
Everything!
You are the source of our life,
our wisdom, our healing.
What have you to do with us, Jesus of Nazareth?
Everything!
You give us mercy, grace, and hope.
What you to do with the world, Jesus of Nazareth?
Everything!
You are the holy one of God,
the savior of the World!
Let us give thanks with our whole hearts!
Amen!

February 4, 2024

Fifth Sunday after the Epiphany

B. J. Beu
Copyright © B. J. Beu

COLOR

Green

SCRIPTURE READINGS

Isaiah 40:21-31; Psalm 147:1-11, 20c;
1 Corinthians 9:16-23; Mark 1:29-39

THEME IDEAS

A celebration of God's power and passion for social justice highlights three of today's readings. Isaiah and the
psalmist proclaim that God is amazing. Have you not
heard it? Have you not seen for yourself how incredible
God is? God is the creator of heaven and earth. God's
power is so awesome, nothing can compare to it. Yet
God cares for the weakest of us. God brings the rulers
of this earth to naught and rescues the downtrodden.
Those who trust God will rise up with wings like eagles.
Jesus, God-with-us, spent much of his ministry healing
the sick and casting out afflicting demons. Let us respond with the psalmist: "Praise the Lord!"

INVITATION AND GATHERING

CENTERING WORDS (Psalm 147)
Those who trust God will rise up with wings like eagles.

CALL TO WORSHIP (Isaiah 40, Psalm 147)
Have you not known? Have you not heard?
Has it not been told to you from the beginning?
The Lord is the everlasting God,
the creator of heaven and earth.
God sits above the circle of the earth
and stretches out the heavens like a curtain.
Those who wait for the Lord
shall mount up with wings like eagles.
They shall run and not be weary.
They shall walk and not faint.
How good it is to sing praises to our God.

OPENING PRAYER (Isaiah 40, Psalm 147)
Everlasting God, you stretch the sky over our heads
like a canopy filled with twinkling lights.
Scarcely do the stems of our lives take root
before the wind carries us away like stubble.
Yet you care for us—
healing the brokenhearted,
gathering the outcast,
lifting the downtrodden,
while casting the wicked to the ground.
Renew our strength this day, O God,
that we may mount up with wings like eagles.
Amen.

PROCLAMATION AND RESPONSE

PRAYER OF YEARNING (Isaiah 40, Psalm 147, Mark 1)
Holy God, even in our pursuit of safety and security,
    we yearn to seek justice for the poor
        and to defend the downtrodden
            from the privilege of the powerful.
Give us the heart of Jesus,
    that we may care for the sick
        and rescue the perishing.
Give us the spirit of Christ,
    that we may spend time in prayer
        and keep your path before our feet.
Give us the love of your Son,
    that we may be instruments of your peace. Amen.

WORDS OF ASSURANCE (Psalm 147)
God showers the earth with rain,
    gives animals their food,
    and offers blessings to those
    who walk in the paths of righteousness.
Sing praises to the Lord
    and rest secure in God's blessings.

PASSING THE PEACE OF CHRIST (Psalm 147)
The one who lifts the lowly and brings down the mighty
offers us a peace that passes all understanding. Claim
the promise of this peace as you share greetings in
Christ's name.

RESPONSE TO THE WORD (Psalm 147)
Rest in God's delight.
Draw strength from God's might and power.
Defend the weak and vulnerable.
Lay claim to the blessings of our God.

THANKSGIVING AND COMMUNION

OFFERING PRAYER (Isaiah 40, Psalm 147)
Creator of heaven and earth,
  you shower the earth with rain,
    nourish the land with sunshine,
      and bless your people with goodness.
Receive the gifts we bring before you this day,
  that they may touch the world with gladness
    and bring succor to those in need. Amen.

SENDING FORTH

BENEDICTION (Isaiah 40)
Though our lives often seem overwhelming,
  in God, we shall mount up with wings like eagles.
Though our responsibilities weigh us down,
  in Christ, we shall run and not be weary.
Though injustice and discord sap our strength,
  in the Spirit, we shall walk and not faint.

February 11, 2024

Transfiguration Sunday

Kirsten Linford

COLOR

White

SCRIPTURE READINGS

2 Kings 2:1-12; Psalm 50:1-6; 2 Corinthians 4:3-6;
Mark 9:2-9

THEME IDEAS

The shared themes in these lections are a study in contrasts: silence vs. speaking, seeing vs. blindness, hearing vs. silence, light vs. shadows, calm vs. storm, faithfulness vs. abandonment. More specifically, what is heard or spoken *in the midst of* what is kept silent; what light or revelation or understanding is found *in the midst of* what is shadowed or veiled, hidden or confused. Taken together, these smaller points lead to a larger one: what faithfulness is possible in the midst of abandonment or change. This seems a fitting precursor to the Lenten season, which commences on the following Sunday. How will transfiguration lead to transformation in the coming season?

INVITATION AND GATHERING

CENTERING WORDS (Psalm 50)
The mighty one speaks and summons the earth from the rising of the sun to its setting. God calls to the heavens and to the earth, "Gather to me my faithful ones."

CALL TO WORSHIP (2 Kings 2, Psalm 50, 2 Corinthians 4)
As we live and as God lives,
God will not leave us.
When fire devours and storms blow us astray,
God will not leave us.
When truth is veiled and confusion reigns,
God will not leave us.
When the world changes around us,
God will not leave us.
When we long to speak but find no words,
God will not leave us.
When all around us is silent,
God will not leave us.
When faithfulness feels beyond us,
God will not leave us.
As we live and as God lives,
we worship the One who will not leave us.

OPENING PRAYER (Psalm 50, 2 Corinthians 4, Mark 9)
Holy One, when the world is full of confusion
and your message is hard to perceive,
still, we can see you.
Still, your presence shines—
a light to illuminate the shadows.
When we cannot find a way to speak your story,
let your being shine in us and through us,
that we may reflect your glory,
and your grace. Amen.

PROCLAMATION AND RESPONSE

PRAYER OF YEARNING (2 Kings 2, Mark 9)
God of life, you never stop shining.
Yet, sometimes we forget to keep looking.
It is not always easy to remember
to keep our eyes on you—
to watch until you are out of sight,
to remember that you are never really
out of sight.
We long for you, O God,
especially when we have wandered away
and yearn to come home.
Entrust us with a double portion of your Spirit—
when we need it most,
when we don't even know we need it,
when we have no words to ask.
Bless us, we pray,
and bring us home. Amen.

*WORDS OF ASSURANCE (2 Kings 2, Psalm 50,
2 Corinthians 4, Mark 9)*
When we have turned away and have lost our way—
still, God is with us;
still, God will not leave us.
When we have stopped looking for God—
God is still looking for us,
shining as brightly as we need,
so we can find and be found
again . . . and again.

PASSING THE PEACE OF CHRIST (2 Corinthians 4)
The one who said, "Let light shine," has shone in our hearts and illumined our lives with knowledge of the glory of God through the face of Jesus Christ. Let us share this grace and peace with one another.

PRAYER OF PREPARATION (Psalm 19)
May the words of my mouth . . .
and the meditations of our hearts
be acceptable in your sight, O Lord,
our strength and our redeemer. Amen.

RESPONSE TO THE WORD (Psalm 50, 2 Corinthians 4, Mark 9)
God, you come and do not keep silent,
no matter the strength of the wind
or the intensity of the fire.
You illuminate our shadows
and bring clarity to our confusion.
You speak.
You shine.
And in your voice, we have heard mercy.
In your presence, we have seen grace.
May your presence, your work, and your Word
move in our minds and hearts,
our bodies and spirits,
to transfigure and transform the world. Amen.

THANKSGIVING AND COMMUNION

INVITATION TO THE OFFERING (2 Kings 2)
As God has given us such a great share of blessings, let us share our gifts with God's people.

OFFERING PRAYER (2 Kings 2, 2 Corinthians 4)
Gracious God, you have given us a double share
of your Spirit . . . and even more . . .
more than we could ask for or ever repay.
You have blessed us with your love
and filled our lives with your grace.

Take now this offering of our hearts and our lives,
that they may be instruments
of your love and your mercy,
your justice and your grace. Amen.

SENDING FORTH

BENEDICTION (*2 Corinthians 4*)
People of God, God has shined life into you.
You have seen it.
Now go and let your lives shine. Amen.

February 14, 2024

Ash Wednesday

James Dollins

COLOR

Purple

SCRIPTURE READINGS

Joel 2:1-2, 12-17; Psalm 51:1-17; 2 Corinthians 5:20b–6:10; Matthew 6:1-6, 16-21

THEME IDEAS

Ash Wednesday offers the invitation to draw close to the Spirit and to be changed during the forty days of Lent. As a sculptor uses negative space to help us see beautiful forms, Lent is a time to subtract so that God may add God's own wisdom to our outlook. Joel calls us to decrease so God may increase, beckoning us to fast and pray. Psalm 51 bids us stop, confess, and speak honestly of our missteps. In 2 Corinthians, Paul speaks honestly about necessary sacrifice and suffering among the faithful. And, in Matthew 6, Jesus calls us to give every gift with genuine humility and love. Let us stop, listen, fast, and pray, so that we may receive all God seeks to give us in the days ahead.

INVITATION AND GATHERING

CENTERING WORDS *(Joel 2, Matthew 6)*
Exhale . . . then inhale the air you need, that you may
fully live and share gifts of life with others.

CALL TO WORSHIP *(Psalm 51)*
People of God, set aside busyness of mind and body.
Create in me a clean heart, O God.
Let us gather in worship with heads unbowed
with shame.
God, put a new and right spirit within me.
Children of God, receive grace from above.
Restore to me the joy of your salvation,
and my mouth will declare your praise!

OPENING PRAYER *(Joel 2, Matthew 6)*
We give thanks, Eternal One,
that we do not walk through life's deserts alone.
You are ever with us,
especially in our loneliest valleys.
You bless us with friends who share this path,
those who wear with us a cross of ashes
to remind us that we are only human.
Quiet the rushing thoughts of our minds.
In this season, may we do less,
so that you may do more.
Receive our songs, our confessions, and our devotion,
until we rise anew with Jesus, alive forevermore.
Amen.

47

PROCLAMATION AND RESPONSE

PRAYER OF CONFESSION or PRAYER OF YEARNING
(Psalm 51, 2 Corinthians 5)
> God of Grace, we give thanks
> > that it is acceptable to be human.
> We rejoice that we do not have to have every answer.
> We praise you that you alone are God.
> May this season of Lent
> > be a time to lament the sin of our world
> > > the suffering of humanity,
> > > > and the travail of creation.
> Reassure us that you have created us "very good,"
> > and that you forgive us when we behave badly.
> May our prayers be honest,
> > trusting you to forgive, heal, and guide us. Amen.

WORDS OF ASSURANCE (Psalm 51)
> The sacrifice acceptable to God is a humble
> > and honest spirit.
> In the name of Jesus Christ, we are forgiven.
> **Thanks be to God. Amen.**

RESPONSE TO THE WORD (Joel 2)
> Even now, return to me with all your heart,
> says the Lord.
> > **In this season of Lent, make God's will our own.**
> Return to me with fasting, weeping, and mourning,
> says our God.
> > **We bring our unanswered questions, laments,**
> > **and confessions to the Holy One.**
> Return to the Lord, your God,
> for God is gracious and merciful.
> > **Return to God who is slow to anger,**
> > **and abounding in steadfast love.**

We dedicate our thoughts, our time, and our work,
that this world may become whole,
beginning with us.

THANKSGIVING AND COMMUNION

OFFERING PRAYER (Joel 2, Matthew 6)
Gracious and generous God, we return these gifts
to you with joyful hearts.
As we share this offering with others,
we make space in our hearts
for your Spirit to fill us,
shape us, and love us.
Bless, Holy Spirit, the gifts we humbly bring,
that they may bring hope to the downcast
and courage to those who live in fear,
for you are the source of all we need. Amen.

SENDING FORTH

BENEDICTION (Joel 2, Psalm 51, Matthew 6)
Walk with God and with one another
through this season of sacrifice and prayer.
Be emptied, then filled, as you are raised with Christ,
now and forevermore. Amen.

February 18, 2024

First Sunday in Lent

Mary Scifres
Copyright © Mary Scifres

COLOR

Purple

SCRIPTURE READINGS

Genesis 9:8-17; Psalm 25:1-10; 1 Peter 3:18-22; Mark 1:9-15

THEME IDEAS

Symbols of hope emerge in today's scriptures. These signs of salvation—rainbows, water, the waters of baptism, doves, and the presence of the Holy Spirit—are central to our faith. They restore our confidence and remind us to place our hope and trust in God, even in the face of despair and tragedy.

INVITATION AND GATHERING

CENTERING WORDS (Genesis 9, Mark 1)

When clouds threaten, look for signs of light and life: a rainbow, a bird, a gentle rain, the waters of baptism. These gifts of love bring hope and wash us clean.

CALL TO WORSHIP (Psalm 25, 1 Peter 3)
Bring your lives, full of sorrow and joy.
Bring yourselves, full of hope and despair.
Come in your brokenness, ready for fullness of life.
Stay in your weakness, ready to receive strength and the power of God.

OPENING PRAYER (Genesis 9, Psalm 25, 1 Peter 3)
Source of hope, bring us into the presence of hope.
Inspire us with the strength of faith.
Shower us with the waters of mercy and grace,
that our hope may be renewed
as we learn to trust your promise and love.
Amen.

PROCLAMATION AND RESPONSE

PRAYER OF YEARNING (Psalm 25, 1 Peter 3)
Merciful God, you know the worries
and the doubts that fill our lives.
Strengthen our faith and inspire our trust.
Shower us with your mercy and grace,
that we may embrace the fullness of life and love,
through the power of your Holy Spirit
and the mercy of Jesus, the Christ. Amen.

WORDS OF ASSURANCE (Psalm 25, 1 Peter 3)
God is good.
All the time.
And all the time,
God is good.
Trust this truth and receive God's gifts
of mercy and love.
Amen.

RESPONSIVE PRAYER (Psalm 25, Mark 1)
I will place my trust in you, O God.
I will place my trust in you.
Help me place my trust in you.
Help me place my trust in you.
I will follow you.
I will follow you.
Help me follow you.
Help me follow you.

THANKSGIVING AND COMMUNION

INVITATION TO THE OFFERING (Genesis 1, Mark 1)
As symbols of love and signs of hope, let us bring our gifts and offerings to God.

OFFERING PRAYER (Genesis 1, Psalm 25)
Trustworthy and trusting God,
thank you for entrusting us with this good earth.
Thank you for sharing your gifts with us.
Help us live up to your trust,
even as we learn to place our trust in you.
Bless the gifts that we share,
that they may honor the generosity
you have shown us.
In trust and gratitude, we pray. Amen.

SENDING FORTH

BENEDICTION (Genesis 9, Mark 1)
Go to be signs of hope for all the world to see:
rainbows in the clouds,
waters in the desert,
love in a world of hate.
Go to be signs of hope for all the world to know.

February 25, 2024

Second Sunday in Lent

Mary Scifres
Copyright © Mary Scifres

COLOR

Purple

SCRIPTURE READINGS

Genesis 17:1-7, 15-16; Psalm 22:23-31; Romans 4:13-25;
Mark 8:31-38

THEME IDEAS

Let go to let God is a theme well-known to twelve-
steppers, though it is a theme far more ancient than
twentieth-century recovery programs. Abram and Sarai
had to let go of former names and paths of despair or they
would never have birthed a family, let alone a nation. By
letting go, they became the parents of Isaac, whose lineage founded many nations of God's followers. Jesus, a
descendent of those nations, calls his followers to die to
their former lives and say "No" to themselves, that God
might change and save our lives. Letting go of the old
to make room for the new, we are invited to trust a future we cannot yet see—a future, nonetheless, that God
holds firmly in hand.

INVITATION AND GATHERING

CENTERING WORDS *(Genesis 17, Romans 4, Mark 8)*
"Let go and let God." This is not just a phrase; it's a life-style. "Die to the old and embrace the new." This is not just a phrase, but a promise of possibilities in God that we often cannot see.

CALL TO WORSHIP *(Genesis 17, Romans 4, Mark 8)*
In promise and covenant, God calls.
In hope and trust, we respond.
In love and faithfulness, God saves.
In gratitude and joy, we come.
Let us worship and praise God's holy name.

OPENING PRAYER *(Genesis 17)*
Ancient of days, bring your future hope into our world.
Bring your love into our lies. ?
Bring your presence into our midst.
Open our hearts and minds to your message,
    that we may respond with hope and trust.
With our ancestors of old,
    may we walk in the lineage of faithful discipleship.
Amen.

PROCLAMATION AND RESPONSE

PRAYER OF CONFESSION *(Genesis 17, Romans 4, Mark 8)*
Faithful One, we want to believe.
Help our unbelief.
We yearn to follow faithfully.
Forgive our hesitant, stumbling steps.
Hold us by the hand, guide us with your love,
    and cover us with your mercy and grace.

Help us answer your call, trust your promises,
    and walk in your ways
        all the days of our lives. Amen.

WORDS OF ASSURANCE (*Romans 4*)

Christ's righteousness has become our righteousness.
God's merciful love is enough to save us.
All is forgiven.
All is restored.
God's beloved are made righteous in Christ's grace.

RESPONSE TO THE WORD (*Genesis 17, Romans 4, Mark 8*)

You are no longer just a name.
You are more than just your past.
Accept the invitation to put pain and regret aside.
    In Christ, we are renewed, and redeemed.
    Following Christ, we are alive and called to love.
    Thanks be to God for this glorious gift!

THANKSGIVING AND COMMUNION

OFFERING PRAYER (*Genesis 17, Romans 4*)

God of ancient days and futures not yet seen,
    bring your eternal wisdom to our time of offering.
Bring your ancient faith and faithful love
    to the gifts we now bring.
Transform the past with the promise of your future,
    that together our gifts may merge with your Spirit
        to bring transformation and hope to your world.
Amen.

SENDING FORTH

BENEDICTION (*Genesis 17, Romans 4, Mark 8*)
Though the former things are past
and the future is unknown,
we go as God's beloved children.
God's love and our place in God's realm is secure,
both now and forevermore.

March 3, 2024

Third Sunday in Lent

Mary Petrina Boyd

COLOR

Purple

SCRIPTURE READINGS

Exodus 20:1-17; Psalm 19; 1 Corinthians 1:18-25; John 2:13-22

THEME IDEAS

God speaks to us through scripture. The Ten Commandments are God's words, revealing God's will for our lives. Psalm 19 rejoices in the gift of God's words and proclaims the voice of the cosmos proclaiming God's glory. First Corinthians reminds us that God's words and God's way might seem foolish to many, but they reveal the deepest truths. As Jesus threw out the money changers, he remembered God's decrees against turning God's house into a marketplace.

INVITATION AND GATHERING

CENTERING WORDS (Psalm 19)
God speaks to our hearts in silence. Be still and touch God's presence.

CALL TO WORSHIP (Psalm 19)
Listen to the stars.
They tell God's glory!
They have no words.
Yet in their beauty, God speaks.
Listen to creation.
It sings God's song of peace.

–OR–

CALL TO WORSHIP (1 Corinthians 1)
Are you wise?
No, not really.
Are you foolish?
Yes, often.
Good! God's foolishness has great power.
We are ready to be fools for God!

OPENING PRAYER (Exodus 20)
Creator God, you call us from our busy lives
to find knowledge and rest in this holy place.
Center our spirits in your love.
Open our hearts to your transforming word,
for we are ready to realign our spirits,
remember your words,
and walk in your paths.
Guide us in wisdom and truth
as we seek to follow your word. Amen.

PROCLAMATION AND RESPONSE

PRAYER OF YEARNING (Psalm 19)
> God of love and truth, we long to walk in your paths.
> We yearn to follow you
>   in the ways that lead to life and wholeness.
> Yet it is hard to know if we are taking the right paths
>   on our journey of faith.
> We worry that we will wander off,
>   even when we don't mean to.
> May your love set us right, forgive our mistakes,
>   and show us where we should go. Amen.

WORDS OF ASSURANCE (Psalm 19)
> God promises forgiveness, that we may be blameless
>   and innocent of any transgression.

INTRODUCTION TO THE WORD (Psalm 19)
> God's words are amazing gifts. In perfection, they revive our weary spirits. In truth, they delight us. Their clarity enlightens us and leads us to wisdom. Let us hear these words with hope and anticipation.

RESPONSE TO THE WORD (Psalm 19)
> God's words are more precious than gold
> and sweeter than honey!
> **Our hearts rejoice in their blessing!**

THANKSGIVING AND COMMUNION

INVITATION TO THE OFFERING (Psalm 19)
> We have heard God's word in the voices of creation and the precepts of scripture. God's word enlightens and revives us, filling us with joy. With grateful hearts, let us bring our gifts before God this day.

OFFERING PRAYER (Exodus 20)
Holy One, you shape our lives with great beauty,
showing us paths that leads to righteousness
and blessing.
We bring these gifts with grateful hearts,
that you may use them to build your community
of justice and righteousness.
We offer you our very lives,
knowing that you will lead us in the path
of holy service. Amen.

GREAT THANKSGIVING (Exodus 20, Psalm 19, John 2)
May God be with you.
May God be with us here.
We come with all we are, body, mind, and spirit.
We offer all we are to God.
Let us thank God.
We thank God for wisdom, truth, and life.

Holy God of wisdom and power,
you alone are worthy of our worship.
At your word, creation came into being:
stars danced, sunlight gleamed on water,
and the earth was filled with growing things.
You gave us your commandments
to guide us in the ways of justice and righteousness.
When we failed to obey your words,
choosing greed and self-interest
over compassion and caring,
your love for us remained steadfast.
You sent prophets to call us back to you,
reminding us that your ways are filled
with abundance.
Your scriptures kept your words before us,
as generations heard your call.

And so, with all of creation,
 and the great company of heaven,
 we praise you as we join in the unending hymn:
 Holy, holy, holy, God of power and strength!
 Creation and heaven are filled with your glory!
 Hosanna in the highest.
 Blessed is Jesus, who comes in your name.
 Hosanna in the highest.

Holy are you, and blessed is your child, Jesus Christ.
In his life and teaching, he showed us your ways.
He welcomed all people, offering forgiveness
 and a new beginning.
He offered healing to aching bodies and spirits.
He shared your kingdom,
 where love and righteousness rule.
Following your laws,
 he dared to challenge places of greed and abuse.

He sat with his friends at the table, sharing a meal,
 knowing that his time was coming.
He took the bread, lifted it to you, and blessed it.
He broke the bread and gave it to his friends, saying:
 "This bread is my life, a gift for you and for many.
 Eat this bread and remember me."
When the meal was over, Jesus took the cup.
He lifted it to you, and giving thanks,
 he offered it to his friends, saying:
 "Drink from this cup.
 This cup represents my love,
 a sign of the new covenant.
 It brings forgiveness from sin
 as it quenches your thirst.
 Drink from this cup and remember me."

And so, we remember Jesus,
    who offered himself in love for us.
We praise you and give thanks
    for all that we have received,
    offering our whole selves to you,
    as we proclaim the mystery of faith.
    Christ was. Christ is. Christ will be.

Pour out your Spirit on those gathered at this table
    and on these gifts of bread and wine.
May they become for us the living Christ,
    renewing us for your work.
May we become the body of Christ,
    sent forth into the world
        as the living presence of love incarnate,
            serving creation with joy.
Transform us in the power of your Spirit
    and unite us with Jesus,
        that we may continue his ministry
            of peace and reconciliation.
Through your child, Jesus Christ,
    with the Holy Spirit in your holy church,
        all honor and glory is yours, Holy God,
            now and forever.
    Amen.

SENDING FORTH

BENEDICTION (1 Corinthians 1)
    God's foolishness is wiser than we will ever know,
        and God's weakness is stronger
            than anything we can imagine.
    Go forth with joyful hearts
        in the foolishness and the weakness of God.
    Go to be a blessing to God's creation.

–OR–

BENEDICTION (1 Corinthians 1)
Go forth as fools for Christ.
Trust in his power and wisdom,
    as you laugh at life.
The world needs holy laughter.

March 10, 2024

Fourth Sunday in Lent

Mary Scifres
Copyright © Mary Scifres

COLOR

Purple

SCRIPTURE READINGS

Numbers 21:4-9; Psalm 107:1-3, 17-22; Ephesians 2:1-10; John 3:14-21

THEME IDEAS

Today's scriptures can feel like a Grimm fairy tale or a warning about Pinocchio's Pleasure Island. A closer look reminds us that judgment and disaster are not the purpose of these scriptures, but salvation and grace. Everyone has faced times of impatience on the road with God. We have all faced temptation and the lure to wander on courses that are best not followed. We have all been bitten by life's difficulties, and we often wonder why. Into these realities, God arrives with the promise of salvation. Christ arrives with the gift of grace. Light emerges, even in the darkest nights and stormiest days, because the storm isn't the end of our story. As Genesis 9 reminded us earlier in Lent, light emerges and a rainbow shimmers through the storm. They are symbols of God's love and grace, letting us know that God is with us through Christ, even in the midst of our trials and tribulations.

INVITATION AND GATHERING

CENTERING WORDS (Ephesians 2, John 3)
Grace is the gift that binds us to God. It protects us, redeems us, restores us, and makes us whole.

CALL TO WORSHIP (Psalm 107, Ephesians 2, John 3)
The goodness of God beckons,
calling us to goodness and grace.
The grace of God redeems,
saving us and making us whole.
The love of God welcomes,
inviting us to worship and praise.

OPENING PRAYER (Psalm 107, Ephesians 2, John 3)
God of goodness and grace,
gather us in your arms of love.
Gather us as people of your goodness and grace.
Gather us in worship and prayer,
that we may be strengthened
with faith and courage.
Gather us as those who are eager to live
and to share your goodness and grace. Amen.

PROCLAMATION AND RESPONSE

PRAYER OF YEARNING (Numbers 21, Psalm 107,
Ephesians 2, John 3)
Gracious God, lift up our hearts this day,
for we long to see your salvation.

Lift us up from the pits of sin and sorrow,
    that we may walk in the light
        of your love and grace.
Create us anew as reflections of your light
    and as offerings of your grace.
For we yearn to bless everyone we meet,
    even ourselves, in your name.
In hope and gratitude, we pray. Amen.

WORDS OF ASSURANCE (Ephesians 2, John 3)
In Christ Jesus, we are created to do good things.
By God's grace, we are able to be good people.
In God's goodness, we are created good.
In Christ's grace, we are saved by love,
    that we may love and be loved.

**RESPONSE TO THE WORD or PASSING THE PEACE
(Ephesians 2)**
You are God's accomplishment.
    You are God's joy.
You are created in Christ Jesus to do good things.
    As are you!
When we live into God's plan,
these good things become our way in the world.
    Goodness and love will be our way of life. Amen.
(Encourage online worshipers to share comments of peace and joy on your video platform. If appropriate, invite all worshipers to take a moment to send a text message of joy and love to someone who isn't in worship today.)

THANKSGIVING AND COMMUNION

INVITATION TO THE OFFERING (Ephesians 2, John 3)
As we have been saved by grace for the goodness of all, may we share our gifts of grace for the goodness of God's world.

OFFERING PRAYER (*Ephesians 2*)
>Merciful God, you have richly blessed our lives
>with love and bounty beyond measure.
>Bless these gifts we return to you now,
>that they may bestow the same richness
>of your love and grace in the world. Amen.

SENDING FORTH

BENEDICTION (*Ephesians 2, John 3*)
>Go forth in the light of God's grace.
>Go forth with the love of Christ's mercy.
>Go forth with the goodness of the Spirit's generosity.

March 17, 2024

Fifth Sunday in Lent

B. J. Beu

COLOR

Purple

SCRIPTURE READINGS

Jeremiah 31:31-34; Psalm 51:1-12; Hebrews 5:5-10;
John 12:20-33

THEME IDEAS

We worship a God of renewal. The prophet Jeremiah proclaims that the days are surely coming when God will make a new covenant with Israel—a covenant written on our hearts, not on parchment or tablets of stone. The psalmist declares that God will put a new and right spirit within us. Jesus proclaims that renewal is neither easy nor free, but requires sacrifice, even death. For unless a grain of wheat dies and is buried, it yields no fruit. The author of Hebrews says that Christ has made the sacrifice necessary for this renewal to take hold in our lives.

INVITATION AND GATHERING

CENTERING WORDS (Jeremiah 31)
God has written the law of love on your heart. Gaze
deeply and find God within.

CALL TO WORSHIP (Psalm 51)
Are you feeling tired and worn out?
Call on the name of the Lord.
Are mistakes from the past weighing you down?
Come to the fount of living water.
Are you the person you wish to be?
Seek God's help and it shall be granted.
Are you looking for a better path?
Ask Christ to show you the way.
Come! Let us worship.

OPENING PRAYER (John 12:24 CEB)
Our souls are troubled, Holy One,
    until they find their rest in you.
When we live in fear of our mortality,
    help us face the future unafraid.
Write the truth of Christ's words on our hearts:
    "Unless a grain of wheat
        falls into the earth and dies,
            it can only be a single seed.
                But if it dies, it bears much fruit."
In our living and in our dying,
    draw us together with all your people. Amen.

PROCLAMATION AND RESPONSE

PRAYER OF YEARNING (Jeremiah 31, Psalm 51)
Engraver of the human heart,
    we long for your law of love to burst forth
        with every beat of our hearts.
Work within us this day,
    that the majesty of your love
        may shine through us
            in everything we say and do.
Put a new and right spirit within us, O Lord,
    that we may leave our failings behind
        and embrace the glory of our salvation,
            through Christ, our Lord. Amen.

WORDS OF ASSURANCE (Jeremiah 31, Psalm 51)
The One who engraves our hearts is faithful,
    remembering our sins no more.
You are loved and accepted,
    for it is written within by our gracious God.

PASSING THE PEACE OF CHRIST (Jeremiah 31, Psalm 51)
With clean hearts and renewed spirits, let us rejoice in
the law of love written on our hearts. Let us share the
peace of Christ with one another.

INTRODUCTION TO THE WORD (John 12)
Jesus prayed that God's name would be glorified, and it
was glorified. As we hear God's word proclaimed this
day, may God be glorified in our midst.

RESPONSE TO THE WORD or BENEDICTION
(Jeremiah 31, John 12)
God writes the ways of life on our hearts.
Look inside and trust what is written there.

Live as those whose hearts are pure.
Love as those whose love is sure.

THANKSGIVING AND COMMUNION

INVITATION TO THE OFFERING *(Jeremiah 31, Psalm 51)*
The One who writes the law of love on our hearts, the
One who saves us from the worst parts of ourselves, is
here to bless us once more. In giving, we receive; in loving, we find love. Let us show our care for those in need
as we offer our tithes and offerings to God.

OFFERING PRAYER *(Jeremiah 31, Psalm 51, John 12)*
With hearts washed clean and with spirits made new,
    we celebrate the joy of your salvation, O God.
May the tithes and offerings we share this day
    reflect the law of love
        you have written on our hearts.
May these gifts bear the fruit of your Spirit,
    and may they bless those who need it most. Amen.

SENDING FORTH

BENEDICTION *(Jeremiah 31)*
God's law of love is engraved on our hearts.
Trust God's internal compass to guide you.
Discern the still small voice
    that whispers with every heartbeat.
Going forth, heed the promise of the heart—
    the warm beat of the living law of love.

March 24, 2024

Palm/Passion Sunday

Mary Scifres
Copyright © Mary Scifres

COLOR
Purple

PALM SUNDAY READINGS
Psalm 118:1-2, 19-29; Mark 11:1-11

PASSION SUNDAY READINGS
Isaiah 50:4-9a; Psalm 31:9-16; Philippians 2:5-11;
Mark 14:1–15:47 or Mark 15:1-39, (40-47)

THEME IDEAS
Humility flows through today's readings, even the celebrative entry into Jerusalem. The path of a joyful parade quickly turned into the Via Dolorosa, reminding us that humility is perhaps the wisest and most difficult guide on any journey. Walking gently and humbly on the journey into Jerusalem, Jesus rode a colt among a crowd that celebrated and honored him. With this same humility, Jesus gathered with his disciples in servanthood and compassion, faced his accusers, and hung on a

cross with criminals. But today, we focus not on the end of the journey, but the entry into Jerusalem at the beginning of holy week. Everything is here—humbleness and triumph—foreshadowing the mystery of death and resurrection yet to come.

(For more ideas related to a Passion Sunday emphasis, see the Good Friday materials.)

INVITATION AND GATHERING

CENTERING WORDS *(Palm Sunday, Mark 11)*
Ride on, King Jesus. Ride with passion and compassion. Ride in triumph and joy. Ride in humility and gentleness. Ride with us as we travel the journey with you.

CALL TO WORSHIP *(Mark 11, Psalm 118)*
In joy, we gather this day.
    Hosanna to Jesus, the Christ.
In remembrance, we gather this day.
    Hosanna to the son of David.
In festive celebration and quiet reflection,
we gather to worship and pray.
    Hosanna to the Son of God.

OPENING PRAYER *(Mark 11, Mark 14-15)*
Jesus, you have walked this road with us many times.
Guide our steps and keep us close.
Inspire our worship with your loving presence
    and work in our lives,
        that your Spirit may flow through our lives
          as we seek to help others
            walk the journey with you. Amen.

PROCLAMATION AND RESPONSE

PRAYER OF YEARNING (Psalm 31, Philippians 2)

Holy One, humble us as we come to you in prayer.
Uncover the masks that obscure our vision
and keep us from facing our true selves.
Hold us close in our weakness,
that we may find the courage to lean on your grace
and rest in your forgiveness.
Bless us with humility, love, and mercy,
that we may be merciful, humble, and loving
to everyone we meet, even ourselves. Amen.

WORDS OF ASSURANCE (Psalm 31, Mark 14-15)

God's face of love shines upon us.
Christ's eyes of forgiveness gaze upon our souls
with mercy and compassion.
The Spirit's sustenance offers us grace and hope,
that we may rise and walk forth in joy.

PASSING THE PEACE OF CHRIST (Psalm 31, Philippians 2)

Be the face of love for your neighbor. Share smiles of
compassion and words of peace as we greet one another
this day.
*(Encourage online worshipers to share comments of peace and
love on your video platform. If appropriate, invite all worshipers to take a moment to send a text message of peace and love
to someone who isn't present in worship today.)*

INTRODUCTION TO THE WORD (Isaiah 50)

May God speak to the weary through today's message.
May God awaken our ears, eyes, hearts, and minds
to receive God's Word.
May God guide our lives and our actions,
as we seek to follow Christ's lead.

RESPONSE TO THE WORD (Mark 11, Mark 14-15, Philippians 2)
>Hosanna to the holy one.
>**Hosanna to the humble one.**
>Hosanna to the courageous one.
>**Hosanna to the loving one.**
>May we take on the cloak of Christ.
>**And may we be holy, humble, courageous, and loving. Amen.**

THANKSGIVING AND COMMUNION

INVITATION TO THE OFFERING (Psalm 118)
>Give thanks to God, who is faithful and good. Give thanks by sharing your tithes and offerings this day.

OFFERING PRAYER (Mark 11, Philippians 2, Mark 14-15, Micah 6:8)
>We thank you, Christ Jesus,
>>for your steadfast faithfulness
>>>and your humble leadership in our world.
>Bless the gifts we return to you now,
>>that they may guide others to follow you
>>>and walk humbly in your ways. Amen.

SENDING FORTH

BENEDICTION (Mark 11, Philippians 2)
>Go into God's world, humble and kind.
>**We will be faithful, courageous, and true.**
>Go into God's world, gracious and loving.
>**We will bring Christ's peace to the world.**

March 28, 2024

Holy Thursday

B. J. Beu
Copyright © B. J. Beu

COLOR

Purple

SCRIPTURE READINGS

Exodus 12:1-4, (5-10), 11-14; Psalm 116:1-4, 12-19;
1 Corinthians 11:23-26; John 13:1-17, 31b-35

THEME IDEAS

Holy Thursday—sometimes called Maundy Thursday, from the mandate Jesus gave his disciples to love one another after he had washed their feet—recalls Christ's celebration of the Passover feast with his disciples on the night before he was crucified. The Passover feast itself recalls the mercy of God, when God passed over the homes of the Hebrew people in Egypt, sparing them from the death of every firstborn in the land. On Holy Thursday, Christ re-images this traditional Passover meal, replacing the sacrificial lamb with his own life, his own body and blood, which became the church's sacrament of Holy Communion. John's account of Holy Thursday includes the foot washing noted above. By washing the feet of his disciples, Christ calls his followers to loving service of one another.

INVITATION AND GATHERING

CENTERING WORDS (John 13)
The promise of love calls. They will know we are Christians by our love.

CALL TO WORSHIP (Psalm 116)
Snares of death surround us.
> **Call on the name of the Lord and be saved.**

Pangs of suffering and grief enfold us.
> **Call on the name of the Lord and be saved.**

Bonds of distress and anguish bind us.
> **Call on the name of the Lord and be saved.**

Come! Let us worship the God of our salvation!

OPENING PRAYER (1 Corinthians 11, John 13)
Your love calls us here, Gracious One,
> calling us to dine with you
>> and to be instruments of your love.

Gather us in Jesus' name,
> that we may offer him the full measure
>> of our devotion. Amen.

PROCLAMATION AND RESPONSE

PRAYER OF YEARNING (Exodus 12)
Eternal God, come to us in our need.
When your people cried out in Egypt,
> you hearkened to their tears.

When Pharaoh refused to let your people go,
>you spared them from death
>>as your plague took Egypt's first born.
When your people today suffer abuse and oppression,
>you hasten to their side.
When the helpless and voiceless are silenced,
>you send prophets to plead their case.
Come and bless us with your never-failing love,
>for we need your power to save us. Amen.

WORDS OF ASSURANCE (Psalm 116, 1 Corinthians 11)
The Lord is the cup of our salvation.
All who call on the name of the Lord will be saved.

PASSING THE PEACE OF CHRIST (John 13)
Christ gave us a new commandment: to love one another.
Let us share this love with one another and find the peace
that comes from sharing Christ's blessing.

RESPONSE TO THE WORD (John 13)
Loving God, help us love one another well.
May we be known as Christ's disciples,
>through the love we share with others.
In this love, may the world be made whole
>in your holy name. Amen.

THANKSGIVING AND COMMUNION

INVITATION TO THE OFFERING (John 13)
Let us bring our offerings to the one who satisfies our
hunger with the bread of life and who quenches our
thirst with the cup of salvation. Let us offer ourselves
and our gifts in loving service, that we may fulfill
Christ's law of love.

OFFERING PRAYER (Psalm 116, John 13)
Source of love and compassion,
  you fill us with a deep spiritual longing
    to taste the cup of salvation
      and to know the joys of servant ministry.
We offer you our very selves
  and the gifts we bring before you now,
    that we may fulfill your law of love
      and be a blessing in our world. Amen.

INVITATION TO COMMUNION (1 Corinthians 11)
Our souls hunger for food that satisfies.
Our spirits long for the bread of heaven.
Taste and see that the Lord is good!
Our souls are dry and parched from thirst.
Our spirits yearn for the cup of salvation.
Taste and see that the Lord is good!

THE GREAT THANKSGIVING (1 Corinthians 11)
The Lord be with you.
  And also with you.
Come to the mountain of the Lord.
  We come to see God's glory.
Lift up your hearts.
  We lift them up to the Lord.
Let us give thanks to the Lord, our God.
  It is right to give our thanks and praise.
It is right, and a good and joyful thing,
  always and everywhere, to give thanks to you,
  almighty God, creator of all things in heaven
  and on earth.
When the earth was formless and void,
  you brought light to the darkness
  and order to the primordial chaos.

From mere clay, you fashioned us in your image,
    and breathed into our lifeless bodies
    the breath of your life-giving Spirit.
When we wandered off and lost our way,
    you sent prophets and teachers
    to show us where we had gone astray.
In the fullness of time, you sent your Son, Jesus Christ,
    to become living water and heavenly food
    for our very souls.
Even at the moment of his darkest hour,
    when the forces of darkness conspired to end his life,
    and his disciples were about to fall away,
    Jesus offered himself as the bread of heaven
    and the cup of our salvation.
And even when we fall away today,
    Christ continues to be for us the bread of heaven
    and the cup of our salvation.
And so, with your people on earth,
    and all the company of heaven,
    we praise your name
    and join their unending hymn, saying:
    Holy, holy, holy Lord, God of power and might,
        heaven and earth are full of your glory.
    Hosanna in the highest. Blessed is the one
        who comes in the name of the Lord.
    Hosanna in the highest.
Holy are you, and blessed is the bread of heaven,
    Christ Jesus.
When you sent Christ to be with us,
    he offered his very self,
    that we might have the strength to stand
    when all hope seems lost.
Through the holy mystery of this table,
    we are invited into your presence,
    tended to in our brokenness,
    and strengthened in our weakness.

With joy and gratitude, we remember that night
    in which Jesus took the bread, broke it,
    and gave it to his disciples, saying:
    "Take, eat, this is the bread of life, given for you.
    Do this in remembrance of me."
After supper, Jesus took the cup, blessed it
    and gave it to his disciples, saying:
    "Drink from this, all of you.
    This is my life in a new covenant,
    poured out for you and for many
    for the forgiveness of sins.
    Do this, as often as your drink it,
    in remembrance of me."
And so, in remembrance of these,
    your mighty acts of love and grace,
    we offer ourselves in praise and thanksgiving.
As your covenant people
    in union with Christ's spirit,
    and as reflections of your glory,
    we proclaim the mystery of faith.
    Christ has died.
    Christ is risen.
    Christ will come again.
(Mary Scifres)

PRAYER OF CONSECRATION (1 Corinthians 11)

Pour out your Holy Spirit on us,
    that we might be servants of others,
        even as Jesus was a servant to his disciples
        and to those in need.
Pour out your Holy Spirit
    on these gifts of bread and wine,
        that they may be for us
        the life and love of Christ;
    and that we may be for the world
        the body of Christ,
            redeemed by your gracious love.

By your Spirit, make us one with Christ,
    one with each other,
        and one in ministry to the world.
In Christ's name, we pray. Amen.

GIVING THE BREAD AND CUP

(The bread and wine are given to the people with these or other words of blessing.)
Take and eat. This is the bread of life.
Take and drink. This is the cup of salvation.

SENDING FORTH

BENEDICTION (Jeremiah 31)

Blessed by God, we are called to live.
Fed by Christ, we are called to serve.
To free us from the cycle of hatred and violence,
    God offers us the promise of Love—
        the promise of a godly future.
Go forth and love one another well.

March 29, 2024

Good Friday

Mary Scifres
Copyright © Mary Scifres

COLOR

Black or None

SCRIPTURE READINGS

Isaiah 52:13–53:12; Psalm 22; Hebrews 10:16-25;
John 18:1–19:42
*(These materials can also be used for a Passion emphasis on
Palm/Passion Sunday.)*

THEME IDEAS

Suffering flows through today's passages, as it has
through our world these last few years. Good Friday allows us a moment to embrace suffering as a reality, both
in our world and in Jesus' life and ministry. We may
feel swamped by the depression and grief that so often accompany suffering. This deep sorrow is reflected
in today's readings and in many of Jesus' words on his
journey to the cross. Even so, there is the hint of a rainbow in the clouds, as the psalmist proclaims trust and
faith in God amid his suffering, and as Isaiah reminds us
that the Suffering Servant will be exalted as the saving

instrument of God's love. Suffering flows through today's story, but it is not the end of the story.

INVITATION AND GATHERING

CENTERING WORDS (Isaiah 52, Isaiah 53, Psalm 22, John 18, John 19)
> God meets us in our suffering. As we sit in the presence of Jesus' suffering, be comforted that it is not the end of his story. Nor is it the end of ours.

CALL TO WORSHIP (Isaiah 52, Isaiah 53, Psalm 22, Hebrews 10, John 18, John 19)
> In sorrow, we gather this day.
> **Even now, we proclaim our hope in Christ.**
> In remembrance of his suffering, we gather to worship.
> **Even now, we find rest in the courage of Christ.**
> In contemplation and reflection, we gather to pray.
> **Our faith and confidence in Christ are sure.**

OPENING PRAYER (Psalm 22)
> God of suffering and sorrow,
> > remind us that we are not alone
> > > in our suffering and our sorrow.
> Open our hearts to Christ's passion,
> > to his suffering and sorrow,
> > > that we may find the wisdom and strength
> > > > to face our own trials and suffering. Amen.

PROCLAMATION AND RESPONSE

PRAYER OF CONFESSION (Psalm 22, Hebrews 10)
> God of comfort and love, be with us amidst our sorrow.
> Draw us near to your love,
> > for we live in a world full of hate and anger.

Grant us the courage, mighty God,
>to endure the trials of this life.
Grant us the faith to embrace hope,
>even in moments of despair.
Sing your Spirit into our lives,
>that we may sing your praises,
>>even on this day of deep grief. Amen.

WORDS OF ASSURANCE (Psalm 22, Hebrews 10)
May those who hunger eat their fill.
May those who suffer find comfort and hope.
God's forgiveness is steadfast and true,
>through the grace and love of Jesus, the Christ.

PASSING THE PEACE OF CHRIST (Hebrews 10)
In this moment of grace, let us share signs of grace and love with one another, that we may encourage one another to find hope in faith.
(Encourage online worshipers to share comments of peace and love on your video platform. If appropriate, invite all worshipers to send a text message of peace and love to someone who isn't present in worship.)

INTRODUCTION TO THE WORD (Isaiah 52, Isaiah 53, John 18, John 19)
Exhale fully, then take a life-giving breath.
Breathe in the power of God's Holy Spirit.
Open yourselves to the harsh reality of Jesus' last days,
>for the tragic story of Jesus' death
>is not the end of his story or ours.

RESPONSE TO THE WORD (*Isaiah 52, Isaiah 53,*
Psalm 22)
>Where there is sorrow,
>>**let us offer comfort and love.**
>Where there is despair,
>>**let us sow seeds of hope.**
>Where there is suffering,
>>**let us work together to bring healing and justice.**
>>**Amen.**

THANKSGIVING AND COMMUNION

INVITATION TO THE OFFERING (*Hebrews 10*)
>Encourage one another to do good works and perform
>acts of loving compassion as we share our tithes and of-
>ferings this day.

OFFERING PRAYER (*Isaiah 52, Isaiah 53, Psalm 22*)
>Bless the gifts we bring before you, Merciful God,
>>that they may comfort those who suffer
>>>and bring hope to those in despair. Amen.

SENDING FORTH

BENEDICTION
>Even as we sit in the presence of death,
>>we do not sit alone.
>Can you sense it?
>Even when we walk in the presence of loss,
>>we are not alone.
>Can you perceive it?
>Hold one another,
>>even as God holds us. Amen.

March 31, 2024

Easter Sunday

Amy B. Hunter

COLOR

White

SCRIPTURE READINGS

Acts 10:34-43; Psalm 118:1-2, 14-24;
1 Corinthians 15:1-11; Mark 16:1-8

THEME IDEAS

We do not prove the resurrection of Jesus Christ, we proclaim it. Our message is more than mere metaphor of the cycle of life or descriptions of recovering things once lost. Easter is our claim that a story of death and defeat is actually the story of eternal life in God. It is our proclamation that God's favor is not for a special few, but for all humanity. Jesus' followers, who betrayed and abandoned him, become witnesses who pass along this good news from generation to generation. We belong to the body of the risen Christ, for we are an Easter people.

INVITATION AND GATHERING

CENTERING WORDS (Psalm 118, Mark 16)
Are you searching tombs and memories for Jesus Christ,
the one who was crucified? Open your eyes to wonder.
Our God is full of surprises.

OPENING (Mark 16:1-8)
(Begin in low light and silence.)
Very early, still in darkness, we set out.
Sorrowful, uncertain, knowing only our loss,
we return to the tomb in our anguish and our love.

Love looks back at us and calls us by name.
You are seeking Jesus, who died on the cross.
He has been raised.
He is not here in your loss.
The tomb could not hold him.
Risen, he goes before you with new life for the world.

(Continue once lights come up and candles are lit.)
Alleluia, Christ is risen!
The Lord is risen indeed! Alleluia!

**CALL TO WORSHIP (Acts 10, Psalm 118,
1 Corinthians 15, Mark 16)**
This very day, God has acted.
Today, we will rejoice and be glad!
We know the message that God sends to all people.
**God's peace, preached by Jesus Christ,
is available to all through the Lord of life.**
The one who lived among us,
doing good and healing all,
was crucified, dead and buried.
But God raised him on the third day.
This very day, God has acted.
Today, we will rejoice and be glad!

OPENING PRAYER (Acts 10, Psalm 118, 1 Corinthians 15)
God, just as you raised Jesus from the dead,
   you offer us new and transformed lives
      in the risen Christ.
We rejoice and give thanks for this good news,
   which has been handed down to us
      from generation to generation.
May we, too, be witnesses of Jesus,
   who you anointed with the Holy Spirit
      to bring blessings of mercy and healing.
May we be witnesses of Jesus' suffering and death,
   and how he meets us in the broken places
      of our lives.
Most of all, may we be witnesses of the resurrection,
   sharing your promise of forgiveness and grace
      with all people.
This is your doing, O God.
It is marvelous in our eyes. Amen.

PROCLAMATION AND RESPONSE

PRAYER OF YEARNING (Acts 10, 1 Corinthians 15, Mark 16)
Risen Jesus, how we long to proclaim the good news
   we have received—
      you are risen,
      the tomb is empty,
         and you are present with your friends.
Remind us not to look for you
   in the places where we lost you—
      our grief,
      our failure,
         the death all around us.

For you have been raised.
You are not trapped in some tomb.
Help us proclaim your resurrection
   with confidence this day.
Flawed as we are, help us perceive
   how deeply we are loved,
      for your grace and mercy never fail. Amen.

WORDS OF ASSURANCE (Acts 10, Psalm 118, 1 Corinthians 15)

Beloved of God, the grace of God is with you,
   and God's grace has not been in vain.
Receive forgiveness and mercy
   through the name of Jesus Christ.

PASSING THE PEACE OF CHRIST (Acts 10)

God sends this message of joy to all people, preaching peace by Jesus Christ, the Lord of all. Let us share this holy peace with one another.

INTRODUCTION TO THE WORD (Acts 10, 1 Corinthians 15)

Hear now the good news of Easter. It spreads throughout the world. It began with Jesus' life, passion, and resurrection; it continued with those who witnessed the risen Christ; and now, it comes to us today, as we listen to God's word.

RESPONSE TO THE WORD (1 Corinthians 15)

Receive the good news handed down by the saints
from generation to generation.
   As the saints have proclaimed the gospel,
   so shall we believe and live it.

THANKSGIVING AND COMMUNION

INVITATION TO THE OFFERING (Psalm 118:1-2, 14-24)
Friends, God has opened the gates of righteousness. Let
us accept God's invitation and offer gifts of thanksgiving in Christ's name.

OFFERING PRAYER (Acts 10, Psalm 118, 1 Corinthians 15)
Holy God, thank you for your goodness and mercy,
especially for the good news
of the resurrection of Jesus Christ.
May these offerings, and indeed our very lives,
become a witness to all people
of the salvation and grace,
you bring into the world. Amen.

SENDING FORTH

BENEDICTION (Psalm 118, Mark 16)
Easter people of Jesus Christ,
this very day, God has acted.
Jesus is raised from the dead.
Let us rejoice and be glad.

April 7, 2024

Second Sunday of Easter

Karin Ellis

COLOR

White

SCRIPTURE READINGS

Acts 4:32-35; Psalm 133; 1 John 1:1–2:2; John 20:19-31

THEME IDEAS

On this Sunday after Easter, we turn our attention to the community. The readings from Acts 4 and Psalm 133 remind us that living in community means taking care of one another and sharing the abundant blessings of God. The readings from 1 John and John 20 give us a glimpse into the life of this new community of faith. In John, the resurrected Christ comes to a frightened community of his disciples and brings them peace. In 1 John, the community proclaims to be witnesses to life in Christ—that is, followers who live in the light of God. May these stories move us and the communities we serve, that we may walk with the resurrected Christ in the light of God.

INVITATION AND GATHERING

CENTERING WORDS or PASSING THE PEACE OF CHRIST (John 20)

> The risen Christ comes to us and says, "Peace be with you." May we lay down the worries of our lives to welcome the peace of Christ.

CALL TO WORSHIP (Psalm 133)

> It is good for God's people to gather together in unity.
> **We are here at the invitation of God.**
> In this place, God's love and grace flow into our lives.
> **In this place, God's blessings abound.**
> Praise be to God!
> **Praise be to God!**

OPENING PRAYER (Psalm 133, 1 John 1, John 20)

> Holy One, we gather with grateful hearts
> > to remember the blessings of your light and love
> > > as they flow through our lives each day.
> In this moment, open our hearts to your Holy Spirit.
> Open our minds to the truths of your story.
> Open our hands to welcome the risen Christ among us.
> And open our eyes to your glory—
> > a glory reflected in the faces around us.
> In the name of the risen Christ, we pray. Amen.

PROCLAMATION AND RESPONSE

PRAYER OF CONFESSION (Acts 4, 1 John 1, John 20)

> God of grace and mercy,
> > we want to continue singing the alleluias of Easter,
> > > but there are days we just don't feel like singing.

Sometimes we lock ourselves away,
    fearful of what has happened
        or what the day may bring.
Sometimes we allow our doubts to overwhelm our faith.
Sometimes we forget about the needs of our neighbors
    because we are so focused on ourselves.
Forgive us.
Draw us back to you and to one another.
Help us walk in your love and light,
    that others may see in us
        the loving presence of the risen Christ. Amen.

WORDS OF ASSURANCE (John 20:23 NRSVUE)

Brothers and sisters, siblings in Christ, Jesus promises:
    "If you forgive the sins of any,
        they are forgiven them."
Receive the hope and promise of this good news,
    for forgiveness is ours when we forgive one another.
Thanks be to God!

PASSING THE PEACE OF CHRIST (John 20)

Peace be with you.
    And also with you.
Receive the Holy Spirit and share the love of the risen
Christ with one another.

PRAYER OF PREPARATION (John 20)

Risen Christ, may the words we speak
    and the stories we hear
        invite us into a deeper relationship with you
            and with one another. Amen.

RESPONSE TO THE WORD (Acts 4, 1 John 1, John 20)

The Holy One is with us this day,
    offering us God's love and light.
The risen Christ is among us,
    inviting us to share what we have seen and heard.

The Holy Spirit guides our way,
> **teaching us to take care of our neighbors,**
and making sure that all are welcomed and loved.
> **Praise be to God!**

THANKSGIVING

INVITATION TO THE OFFERING (Psalm 133)
> The love and light of God flow through our lives, bring-ing us joy and hope. With thanksgiving in our hearts, let us offer our gifts to God, the source of all our blessings.

OFFERING PRAYER (Psalm 133, Acts 4)
> Abundant God, we are grateful for all your blessings,
>> especially for the presence of the risen Christ.
> Bless these gifts,
>> that they may help bring your love and light
>>> into our community and our world. Amen.

SENDING FORTH

BENEDICTION (John 20)
> Brothers and sisters, siblings in Christ,
>> may the love of God, the peace of the risen Christ,
>> and the power of the Holy Spirit
>> fill your hearts, now and always. Amen.

April 14, 2024

Third Sunday of Easter

Mary Scifres
Copyright © Mary Scifres

COLOR

White

SCRIPTURE READINGS

Acts 3:12-19; Psalm 4; 1 John 3:1-7; Luke 24:36b-48

THEME IDEAS

Today's scriptures remind us that witnesses to the mighty power of resurrection and new life in Christ Jesus are called to become instruments of God's mighty power of resurrection and new life in Christ Jesus. We, who have witnessed God's miraculous love and impact in our lives, are empowered and challenged to bring this love and impact to the world—even when the world rejects and doubts us.

INVITATION AND GATHERING

CENTERING WORDS (*Acts 3, Psalm 4, 1 John 3, Luke 24*)
Trust God. Trust the miracles you have known. Trust the miracle you can be.

CALL TO WORSHIP (Acts 3, Psalm 4)
Turn to Christ,
   who calls us here.
Place your trust in God,
   who protects our lives.
Lean into Spirit,
   as we worship in Spirit and truth.

OPENING PRAYER (Acts 3, Luke 24)
God of miracles and truth,
   bless us, as we gather for worship,
      with the power of your Holy Spirit.
Reveal your presence in our midst
   and open our hearts and minds
      to receive your miraculous love.
Strengthen our faith this day,
   that we may go forth as witnesses
      of your miraculous love. Amen.

PROCLAMATION AND RESPONSE

CALL TO CONFESSION (Acts 3)
Turn to God.
If your heart is heavy,
   invite Christ to lighten the load.
If your hearts is hardened,
   invite the Spirit to soften and change you.
Truly, we all need to receive God's grace
   and to heed Christ's call.

PRAYER OF YEARNING (Acts 3, Psalm 4)
Answer us, O God, as we turn to you
   for mercy and strength.
Listen to the yearnings of our hearts
   and the regrets of our lives.

Comfort us in our distress
and pour your grace into our lives.
Redeem us with your love,
that we might rise with Christ,
newborn and vibrantly alive.
Grant us the confidence
to witness to your life-giving love. Amen.

WORDS OF ASSURANCE (Acts 3, Psalm 4)
God fills our hearts with joy
and covers our lives with grace.
Rest in this truth and be at peace.
All is well and all will be well.

PASSING THE PEACE OF CHRIST (Psalm 4, Psalm 23)
As God leads us beside the still waters of grace, Christ
invites us to offer these still waters of grace and peace to
one another, that all may know the peace of God.
(If you have safety protocols that limit personal interaction in
worship and as an online worship practice, encourage people
to send personal greetings of peace, love, and grace via social
media, email, text, phone, or snail mail.)

RESPONSE TO THE WORD (Acts 3, Luke 24)
Who will be a witness?
We will be a witness.
What will we witness?
The truth of God's love.
To whom will we witness?
Everyone we meet.

THANKSGIVING AND COMMUNION

INVITATION TO THE OFFERING (1 John 3)

As we have been loved, we are invited to love. As God has given generously to us, we are invited to give generously to God and to God's church. May our hearts brim with love and generosity for all as we enter this time of offering.

OFFERING PRAYER (Acts 3, 1 John 3, Luke 24)

Generous God of love and grace,
> bless these gifts with your abundant love
> and your life-giving grace.
Bless us as we bear witness to your love and grace
> in all that we say, all that we give,
> and all that we do. Amen.

SENDING FORTH

BENEDICTION (Acts 3, 1 John 3, Luke 24)

You are witnesses of God's love.
We are witnesses of God's love.
You are witnesses of Christ's life.
We are witnesses of Christ's life.
You are witnesses of the power of the Holy Spirit.
We are witnesses of life and love in the Spirit.
Go forth as witnesses of the blessings of our God.

April 21, 2024

Fourth Sunday of Easter

Sara Lambert

COLOR

White

SCRIPTURE READINGS

Acts 4:5-12; Psalm 23; 1 John 3:16-24; John 10:11-18

THEME IDEAS

The stone that was rejected becomes the building's cornerstone in the Acts passage. Despite his crucifixion, Jesus is salvation for all humanity. In beloved Psalm 23, the Lord is represented as a shepherd, foreshadowing the Good Shepherd of the Gospels. The psalmist reminds us to seek comfort and restoration, since all are welcome to the table of the Lord. John 10 and 1 John 3 return us to abide in Christ's resurrection—Christ laid down his life for us, so we must follow his lead. Following the model of Christ, we are to act with charity and love in the world.

INVITATION AND GATHERING

CENTERING WORDS (Acts 4, 1 John 3, Psalm 23, John 10)
Be bold before God, for Christ, the rejected one, has become the cornerstone of our faith. Through the Good Shepherd, you are found, comforted, and loved.

CALL TO WORSHIP (Psalm 23, 1 John 3, John 10)
The Lord is my shepherd, I will fear no darkness.
We will love one another, as Christ loves us.
Christ, the Good Shepherd, has compassion for all.
We will love one another, as Christ loves us.
Open your hearts to goodness and mercy today.
We will love one another, as Christ loves us.
Love, not merely in thought and word,
but in truth and action.
We will love one another, as Christ loves us.

–OR–

CALL TO WORSHIP (1 John 3, Psalm 23)
Are we eager to show Christ's love for one another
in truth and action?
Are we ready to study the example of Jesus,
who laid down his life for us?
As we consider how to absorb God's lessons,
may we bring others to Christ's fold.

OPENING PRAYER
Shepherding God, guardian of our souls,
you offer us rest in the safety of green pastures.
Shower us with your love,
and offer us fullness of life in your name.
When our spirits are parched,
you lead us beside still waters
and quench our thirst for righteousness;

you restore our souls
and heal our battered spirits.
Touch our hearts and minds,
that your goodness and mercy may follow us
every day of our lives.
May we abide in your love and grace
for all eternity. Amen.
(B. J. Beu)

PROCLAMATION AND RESPONSE

PRAYER OF YEARNING (Acts 4, 1 John 3, Psalm 23, John 10)
Good Shepherd, help us become your bold acolytes,
lighting the way of your truth for all to see.
Help us choose honorable paths
through green pastures and still waters
amid the darkest valleys of our lives.
For you are greater than our fears
and you know how to bring us peace.
As you laid down your life for us,
may we strive to live for others.
We choose you this day,
for no other name under heaven
inspires us to greater joy. Amen.

WORDS OF ASSURANCE (Psalm 23, Acts 4, John 10)
You are welcome at the table of the Lord.
The Good Shepherd beckons all to come
and be restored.
Rejoice in the knowledge that you are loved!

PASSING THE PEACE OF CHRIST (Psalm 23, 1 John 3)
May the peace of Christ make you ready for love to
flow around and through you. May you boldly share

his love as you pass the peace of Christ with one another this day.

RESPONSE TO THE WORD *(Psalm 23, 1 John 3, John 10)*
Good Shepherd, show us your path
through the peaks and valleys of our lives.
May goodness and mercy flow through us,
as your love sparks our actions.
Help us put our whole selves into the world
as we seek to walk in your truth and love.
You are our shepherd,
today, tomorrow, and always. Amen.

THANKSGIVING AND COMMUNION

OFFERING PRAYER *(Psalm 23, John 10)*
As the Good Shepherd lays down his life for his sheep,
may we, too, strive to serve our neighbors.
Whether next door, across town, or around the world,
may God bless our prayers, our gifts,
and our ministries.
In Christ's name, we present these gifts. Amen.

SENDING FORTH

BENEDICTION *(1 John 3, John 10)*
May you show boldness before God in all you do.
Following Jesus Christ, the Good Shepherd,
act with kindness, love, and humility.
Bring comfort to others, acting with love and truth.

April 28, 2024

Fifth Sunday of Easter

Mary Scifres
Copyright © Mary Scifres

COLOR

White

SCRIPTURE READINGS

Acts 8:26-40; Psalm 22:25-31; 1 John 4:7-21; John 15:1-8

THEME IDEAS

Today's scriptures challenge us to remain in God. Christ
promises to be the vine that will strengthen us, as long
as we are connected to him. John's letter clarifies that
our connection is bonded by love. Remain in God, by remaining in love. Remain in Christ, by sharing the good
news of God's love, whether by witnessing and teaching, as Phillip did, or by caring for a brother or sister,
as John advises. In this love, we remain in Christ and
Christ remains in us.

INVITATION AND GATHERING

CENTERING WORDS (1 John 4, John 15)
Connected to Christ through the power of love, we become the presence of God for the world.

CALL TO WORSHIP (1 John 4, John 15)
As members of Christ's tree of life,
we are connected, in love, to God.
As members of Christ's tree of life,
we are connected, in love, to one another.
As members of Christ's tree of life,
we strengthen our connection through worship.

OPENING PRAYER (Acts 8, 1 John 4, John 15)
Loving God, send your Spirit among us now.
Bind us to you in love this day,
that we may worship in unity and friendship.
Bind us to you in love this hour,
that we may be strengthened
to bring abundant love to your world.
In love and gratitude, we pray. Amen.

PROCLAMATION AND RESPONSE

PRAYER OF CONFESSION (Acts 8, Psalm 22, 1 John 4, John 15)
Speak truth to our hearts, O God.
Speak love to our lives,
that we may remain in your love
and share your love joyously with others.
Speak grace to our souls,
that we may rest in your grace
and forgive others as we have been forgiven.

Speak mercy to our world,
    that all the world may know your love
        and find redemption in your grace.
In hope and trust, we pray. Amen.

WORDS OF ASSURANCE (Psalm 22, 1 John 4)

God's promises are sure.
The promises of forgiveness, grace, and love are true.
In Christ's love and grace,
    we are forgiven and made new.

PASSING THE PEACE OF CHRIST (1 John 4)

Abiding in God's love, let's share signs of love and peace
with one another.
*(Encourage online worshipers to share comments of peace and
joy on your video platform. If appropriate, invite all worshipers to take a moment to send a text message of joy and love to
someone who isn't in worship today.)*

RESPONSE TO THE WORD (Acts 8, Psalm 22, 1 John 4)

Loving God, send your Spirit to guide us,
    as you guided Philip long ago.
Guide us to listen,
    when people cry out for understanding.
Guide us to speak,
    when people yearn for your good news.
Guide us to compassion,
    when people reach out for help.
Guide us to love,
    when people curl up from loneliness.
Send your Spirit to guide us,
    that we may open our hearts and minds
        to hear and heed your guidance. Amen.

THANKSGIVING AND COMMUNION

INVITATION TO THE OFFERING (1 John 4, John 15)
Connected in love, let us share our love offerings with
Christ's church and God's world.

OFFERING PRAYER (1 John 4, John 15)
Loving God, bless these gifts with love.
Transform lives with our ministries,
  that your people everywhere
  might know your grace,
    abide in your love,
      and connect with Christ,
        the vine of life. Amen.

SENDING FORTH

BENEDICTION (1 John 4, John 15)
As God's children, go now to serve.
We go to serve in love.
Abiding in Christ, go with Christ to love.
We go with Christ's love to love one another.
Go to serve in love and peace.

May 5, 2024

Sixth Sunday of Easter

Kirsten Linford

COLOR

White

SCRIPTURE READINGS

Acts 10:44-48; Psalm 98; 1 John 5:1-6; John 15:9-17

THEME IDEAS

All four lections speak to the greatest victory known on earth—not the defeat of an enemy but the power of love. Such love, and the presence of God's very Spirit, are meant for all—Jews and Gentiles, those nearby and those faraway, and those who are as different from one another as they could be. God's love and presence are a message for all creation, and they are a fitting message for the Easter season and for a Sunday closely following Earth Day. As we have been actively loved by God, so are we called to love, in word and action.

INVITATION AND GATHERING

CENTERING WORDS (Psalm 98, John 15)

The Holy One's steadfast love and faithfulness are shared with all. We are called to the greatest commandment: to abide in God's love and to love one another as God has loved us—not as servants, but as friends.

CALL TO WORSHIP (Psalm 98)
Sing to our God a new song,
for God has done wondrous things.
The Holy One's might is not found in destruction,
but in steadfast love and constant faithfulness.
These gifts are not for us alone,
they are for one and all.
Make a joyful noise to the Lord, all the earth.
Break forth into songs of praise.
Let all creation praise the Lord.

OPENING PRAYER (Acts 10, John 15)
God of Love, let your Holy Spirit come upon us—
into our hearts,
into our minds,
and into our souls.
Let your presence speak within us—
in the languages we speak,
in the ways we live and have our being.
For we long to hear you, Gracious One,
and to understand.
We pray that you would abide in us,
that we may abide in you,
this day and all days. Amen.

PROCLAMATION AND RESPONSE

PRAYER OF YEARNING (Acts 10, Psalm 98, 1 John 5)
O God, you are bigger than the world,
bigger than our fears,
bigger even than our folly.
We are grateful for the immensity of your love,
even when it sometimes scares us.

When the immensity of your love frightens us,
    we long to return to you in hope.
When we want to make you smaller—
    small enough that we can hold you—
        help us see beyond our narrow vision.
Remind us again, O God,
    that you will always find and hold us,
        for your heart is big enough
            to hold the whole world, including us.
Teach us once more that we will always grow
    when we love others as we love you. Amen.

WORDS OF ASSURANCE (Acts 10, Psalm 98, 1 John 5)

The God of mercy speaks every language.
When we open our ears,
    we hear and receive God's grace.
Whenever we are afraid or overwhelmed,
    we have only to remember these truths.
God's love is the greatest power of all.
God's mercy is there for every one of us.
God's grace is present every moment
    of our lives. Amen.

PASSING THE PEACE OF CHRIST (John 15)

As God has loved us, so shall we love each other. As Christ has called us friends, so we have become friends to one another. Let us abide in God's love together now, sharing both friendship and peace.

PRAYER OF PREPARATION (Psalm 19)

May the words of my mouth . . .
    and the meditations of our hearts
        be acceptable in your sight, O Lord,
            our strength and our redeemer. Amen.

RESPONSE TO THE WORD (Acts 10)

Like our ancestors in faith before us,
    we have heard the Word
        and received the Spirit.
May your Word and your presence
    work within us, O God.
May they come to life
    through our lives. Amen.

THANKSGIVING AND COMMUNION

INVITATION TO THE OFFERING (Acts 10)

The Holy Spirit's gifts have been poured into our hearts
and our lives. In response, let us share these blessings
for the good of God's people.

OFFERING PRAYER (Acts 10, Psalm 98, John 15)

O God, our hearts sing with thanksgiving
    for the many gifts and graces
        you bring to our lives.
We give you thanks for your steadfast love
    and faithful Spirit.
Receive this offering
    and the gift of our whole selves,
        that we might give as we have received
            and love as we have been loved. Amen.

SENDING FORTH

BENEDICTION (Psalm 98, John 15)

People of God, abide in God's love.
May God's love and faithfulness flow through you,
    even to the ends of the earth. Amen.

May 12, 2024

Ascension of the Lord/Mother's Day

Mary Scifres
Copyright © Mary Scifres

COLOR

White

SCRIPTURE READINGS

Acts 1:1-11; Psalm 47; Ephesians 1:15-23; Luke 24:44-53

ALTERNATE SCRIPTURE READINGS FOR THE SEVENTH SUNDAY AFTER EASTER

Acts 1:15-17, 21-26; Psalm 1; 1 John 5:9-13; John 17:6-19

THEME IDEAS

As the Easter season comes to a close, we are reminded that just as Christ was sent to earth with heavenly power to change lives and share God's message, Christ's disciples are also sent with heavenly power to continue this call. The ascension of Christ opened the path for God's glory and power to descend upon those remaining behind. Throughout these various scriptures, Jesus commands the disciples to await the Spirit's power and then go forth in answer to this call. Paul prays for us to be enlightened with the hope of this call; and the psalmist calls us to pursue our inherited call as followers of God with patience and steadfast faithfulness.

INVITATION AND GATHERING

CENTERING WORDS *(Acts 1, Luke 24, John 17)*
Why stare at the heavens to find God? Look within, for God's Spirit is there. Look around, for Christ's disciples are all around.

CALL TO WORSHIP *(Psalm 47, Ephesians 1)*
Clap your hands and sing for joy!
Christ is in our midst and in our lives.
Clap your hands and sing for joy!
Christ calls us to worship and praise.
Let's worship together.

OPENING PRAYER *(Acts 1, Luke 24, John 17)*
Risen Christ, be present in our lives
    and in our worship.
Help us recognize and celebrate your presence.
Grant us the power of your Holy Spirit,
    that we may answer the call to be your disciples
        and bring your message of love to the world.
Amen.

PROCLAMATION AND RESPONSE

PRAYER OF YEARNING *(Acts 1, Ephesians 1, Luke 24, John 17)*
Great and glorious God,
    we are tired of thinking small.
When we look for you in all the wrong places,
    remind us that your Spirit resides within.

When we shy away in shame and regret,
    help us sense the fullness of your grace.
Lift our eyes to your glorious presence in our midst,
    that we may reflect your glory and grace
        for all to see. Amen.

WORDS OF ASSURANCE (Ephesians 1, John 17)
In Christ's love, we are loved.
In Christ's glory, we are glorified.
In Christ's grace, we are saved.
Amen.

RESPONSE TO THE WORD (Acts 1, Ephesians 1, Luke 24, John 17)
Why look above?
Look around and look within;
    the world needs our gifts.
This is the hope to which we are called.
How might we await the Spirit's power?
How might we respond to God's call?
Look around and look within;
    the world needs our gifts.

THANKSGIVING AND COMMUNION

INVITATION TO THE OFFERING (Psalm 47)
With songs of joy and hearts of love, let us bring our offerings and gifts in gratitude to God.

OFFERING PRAYER (Luke 24)
Glorious God, may these gifts bring glory to you
    and grace to your world.
May our lives and our ministry reflect your love,
    and may we spread your message of love
        throughout the world. Amen.

SENDING FORTH

BENEDICTION (Psalm 47, Ephesians 1, Luke 24)
Go forth with joy.
Go forth with hope.
Go forth with Christ's love leading the way.

May 19, 2024

Pentecost Sunday

B. J. Beu
Copyright © B. J. Beu

COLOR

Red

SCRIPTURE READINGS

Acts 2:1-21; Psalm 104:24-34, 35b; Romans 8:22-27;
John 15:26-27; 16:4b-15

THEME IDEAS

As Jesus' disciples huddled together in fear, the Holy
Spirit entered their dwelling in rushing wind and tongues
of fire. From that event, the Church was born. Without
Pentecost, the disciples would not have had the courage
to go forth and spread the gospel. Without Pentecost, the
Spirit promised to the prophet Joel would not be the active force it is in our world today—granting visions and
dreams to old and young alike. God's power to create
and renew life is the power of the Holy Spirit. We see this
power in the psalmist's hymn of praise. We behold this
power in Paul's discussion of adoption in Christ through
the Spirit. And we see the promise of this power in Jesus,
as he comforts his disciples before his death.

INVITATION AND GATHERING

CENTERING WORDS (Acts 2)

In rushing wind and tongues of fire, the Church is born
through the power of the Holy Spirit.

CALL TO WORSHIP (Acts 2, John 14)

In rushing wind and tongues of fire . . .
the Church is born.
In courage found and faith renewed . . .
the Church gains strength.
In visions seen and dreams made real . . .
the Church blesses the world.
In hopes rekindled and fears released . . .
the Church leads the way.
In rushing wind and tongues of fire . . .
Come, Holy Spirit, come.

OPENING PRAYER (Acts 2)

God of wind and flame, ignite a fire in our hearts
and fill us with your courage and power.
On this day of Pentecost,
may our young people see visions
and our elders dream dreams.
Blow open the doors of our shut up hearts
and send us into the world
to spread the good news of your saving love.
Amen.

PROCLAMATION AND RESPONSE

PRAYER OF YEARNING (Acts 2, Psalm 104, Romans 8)

Creator God, the earth is full of your creatures.
When you send forth your spirit,
they are created.

When you take away their breath,
  they return to the earth.
Open your hand and fill us with good things, Holy One,
  that we may sing and rejoice in your presence.
Save us from our weakness and intercede on our behalf,
  that we may proclaim the glory of your world
    and help others claim your many blessings.

Words of Assurance (Psalm 104, Romans 8)
  God searches the heart
    and the Spirit helps us in our weakness.
  Rejoice, sisters and brothers in Christ,
    God's steadfast love endures forever.

PASSING THE PEACE OF CHRIST (John 15)
  God sent the Advocate to seal the blessings of Christ in
  our lives. Let us claim these blessings for ourselves and
  for one another as we share signs of Christ's peace.

INTRODUCTION TO THE WORD (Acts 2)
  From fear and doubt, the Spirit blessed Christ's disciples with a faith so deep that it birthed the church and
  changed the world. As we listen for the word of God in
  today's scripture, may the Spirit bless us and continue
  to change the world.

RESPONSE TO THE WORD (Acts 2, Romans 8)
  All who bear the first fruits of the Spirit
  are children of God's hope.
    We are heirs of God's redeeming love.
  All who wait with patience for the hope of our salvation
  are saints of the living God.
    We are heirs of the Spirit, who intercedes for us
    with sighs too deep for words.
  All who see God's visions and dream God's dreams
  have the power to change the world.
    Thanks be to God.

THANKSGIVING AND COMMUNION

INVITATION TO THE OFFERING (Psalm 104)
When the Spirit extends a hand, we are filled with good things. When our breath is taken away, we return to the earth. In the time we have, let us share God's bounty to the glory of our maker and for the blessing of our world.

OFFERING PRAYER (Acts 2, Romans 8)
Merciful God, the blessings of Pentecost
continue to birth hope for the future
and offer blessings for those in need.
May today's offering bring love and light
to those who have yet to touch the holy wind
and sacred fire of your Spirit. Amen.

SENDING FORTH

BENEDICTION (Acts 2, John 15)
In rushing wind and cleansing fire,
go forth in the power of the living God.
We go as children of God.
In courage found and strength renewed,
go forth in the power of the eternal Christ.
We go as heirs with Christ.
In visions born and dreams restored,
go forth in the power of the Holy Spirit.
We go as new creations in the Spirit.

May 26, 2024

Trinity Sunday

B. J. Beu
Copyright © B. J. Beu

COLOR

White

SCRIPTURE READINGS

Isaiah 6:1-8; Psalm 29; Romans 8:12-17; John 3:1-17

THEME IDEAS

Trinity Sunday is a time to celebrate the fullness of God in the persons of the Father, Son, and Holy Spirit. The God Isaiah experiences face-to-face in the Temple is the same God that Paul proclaims as the Father of Jesus Christ—the One who adopts us as children of God through the power of the Holy Spirit. This triune God is the one revealed by Christ when he was lifted up to bring us eternal life. The inner life of God is so holy and awe-inspiring that we are truly born from above when we are brought into communion with the Holy One.

INVITATION AND GATHERING

CENTERING WORDS

With strength and power, the Father comes to us. With arms stretched wide, the Son calls to us. With sighs too deep for words, the Spirit heals us. Thanks be to God, Mother and Father of us all.

CALL TO WORSHIP (Psalm 29)

Who is like our God in glory and strength?
The voice of the Lord thunders over the waters.
Who is like the Lord in power and might?
The voice of God breaks the mighty cedars.
Who is like the Holy One in awe and wonder?
The voice of the Almighty shakes the wilderness.
God sits enthroned as King forever.
Worship God in holy splendor.
Come! Let us worship the Lord.

OPENING PRAYER (Psalm 29, Romans 8, John 3)

Your Spirit calls us here, O God,
to behold the glory of your majesty and power.
For adopting us into your family
and making us heirs with Christ,
we thank you.
For freeing us from the failings of the flesh,
that we may be born anew
with water and the Spirit,
we praise you. Amen.

PROCLAMATION AND RESPONSE

PRAYER OF YEARNING (Isaiah 6)
God of power and might,
    we long to proclaim your glory
        with the seraphs and angels,
    yet your holiness is more than we can bear.
We yearn to feel worthy of your calling,
    but often feel naked and lost
        when confronted with your majesty.
Touch our mouths with coal from your sacred fire,
    for we are a people with unclean lips
        and long to be made clean.
Above all, heal our shut up hearts, O God,
    that we may say with the prophet Isaiah,
        "Here I am, send me." Amen.

WORDS OF ASSURANCE (Romans 8)
Rejoice that God heals our fear
    with a spirit of strength and truth.
Give thanks that we are God's children
    and heirs with Christ.
In Christ, we touch God's glory and victory.

PASSING THE PEACE OF CHRIST (Romans 8)
Adopted with Christ into the family of God, let us offer
thanks and praise as we share signs of Christ's peace
today.

INTRODUCTION TO THE WORD (Romans 8)
Hear the word of God, seekers of the way,
for God has called us to this moment.
    The Spirit has led us here
    to deepen our faith and understanding.

Hear and rejoice, children of God,
for God has made us heirs with Christ.
We are adopted into Christ's family,
and we are glorified with him.
Hear and be free, children of promise,
for the Spirit allays our fears.
We will hear and heed God' holy word.

RESPONSE TO THE WORD *(John 3)*
Be born of water and the Spirit.
In Christ and the Spirit, we are born anew.
Rejoice in the blessings of everlasting life.
In God, we receive glory and salvation.
Worship God, the three in one.

THANKSGIVING AND COMMUNION

OFFERING PRAYER *(Romans 8, John 3)*
Spirit of the living God, you offer us rich blessings
and a church family to guide our way.
We are your children,
eager to show you our gratitude and our love.
May this offering be a sign of our commitment
to live as brothers and sisters of Christ.
Bless our gifts this day, O God,
that others may be blessed by them.
May they help those in need
be born anew in your Spirit
and blessed in your holy name. Amen.

SENDING FORTH

BENEDICTION *(Isaiah 6)*

Who will go to serve our God?
> **Even when we feel fearful,**
> **we will go to serve the Lord.**

Who will go to serve our neighbors?
> **Even when we feel unworthy,**
> **we will go to serve our sisters and brothers.**

Who will go to serve our world?
> **Even when we feel unprepared,**
> **we will go to serve God's people.**

We are your servants, Lord.
> **Send us.**

June 2, 2024

Second Sunday after Pentecost
Proper 4

B. J. Beu
Copyright © B. J. Beu

COLOR

White

SCRIPTURE READINGS

1 Samuel 3:1-20; Psalm 139:1-6, 13-18;
2 Corinthians 4:5-12; Mark 2:23–3:6

THEME IDEAS

God is full of surprises. Samuel is surprised to find himself called at such a young age. The psalmist is surprised
to be known so completely and to be so fearfully and
wonderfully made. The epistle writer is surprised that
the power to shine God's light resides within us. And
Jesus is surprised that the gift of the Sabbath is used as a
weapon against God's own people. May we continue to
be surprised, and may we use this surprise to continue
God's work in the world.

INVITATION AND GATHERING

CENTERING WORDS (Psalm 139)
Before we speak, God knows our thoughts and minds completely, calling us into fellowship this day.

CALL TO WORSHIP (2 Samuel 3, Psalm 139, 2 Corinthians 4:6 NRSVUE)
The One who called Samuel from the darkness
continues to say: "Let light shine out of darkness."
The light of Christ shines all around us.
The One who searches us and knows us
hems us in, behind and before.
We are fearfully and wonderfully made.
Let us worship a God who surprises us at every turn.

OPENING PRAYER (Mark 2–3)
Merciful One, when life beats us down,
    you reach out and restore us to health
        and wholeness.
Surprise us once more, O God,
    with your never-failing grace
        and the light of your love. Amen.

PROCLAMATION AND RESPONSE

PRAYER OF YEARNING (Mark 2–3)
Lord of the Sabbath, when our spirits feel withered,
    we yearn to touch your healing power.
Be with us in our hour of need
    and become the joy of our salvation.
Our mouths long to sing your praise
    and our eyes long to behold your glory.
In your holy name, we pray. Amen.

WORDS OF ASSURANCE *(Psalm 139, 2 Corinthians 4)*
Though we are but vessels of clay,
    the extraordinary power of God
        shines light in and through our darkness.
Though our span of years is short,
    we are fearfully and wonderfully made.
God blesses us with mercies beyond measure.

PASSING THE PEACE OF CHRIST *(Mark 2–3)*
The Lord of the Sabbath invites us to reach out to one another and share his blessing of peace this day.

INTRODUCTION TO THE WORD *(1 Samuel 3, Psalm 139)*
As we listen for the word of God, may we be prepared to respond as inspired prophets, humble servants, and faithful disciples.

RESPONSE TO THE WORD OR BENEDICTION
(Mark 2–3, 2 Corinthians 4)
Receive the blessings of Sabbath rest this day.
    We will stretch out our hands
    and touch Christ's healing love.
The light of God illumines our path
and guides our way.
    We will walk in the light of God
    and share the blessings of the Lord.

THANKSGIVING AND COMMUNION

INTRODUCTION TO THE OFFERING *(Psalm 139,*
2 Corinthians 4)
As those who are fearfully and wonderfully made, let us share the blessings of our maker with those who need God's light and glory in their lives.

OFFERING PRAYER (Mark 2–3, 2 Corinthians 4)
Though we are vessels of clay,
your light shines through us
when we share what we have
with those in need.
May today's offering be like the bread of presence
that feeds the hungry and satisfies the soul.
In Christ's name, we pray. Amen.

SENDING FORTH

BENEDICTION (Psalm 139, Mark 2–3)
The extraordinary power of God leads us
on our journeys of faith.
With the blessings of Sabbath rest
and the healing of God's love,
go to be a blessing.
Go as those who are fearfully and wonderfully made.

June 9, 2024

Third Sunday after Pentecost
Proper 5

B. J. Beu
Copyright © B. J. Beu

COLOR

Green

SCRIPTURE READINGS

1 Samuel 8:4-20, (11:14-15); Psalm 138;
2 Corinthians 4:13–5:1; Mark 3:20-35

THEME IDEAS

How do we build something that will endure? Do we put our trust in human families, in human ingenuity and cleverness, or do we put our faith in God? God came to the boy Samuel, pronouncing judgment against the house of Eli because his sons had blasphemed against the Lord. In today's reading, the elders of Israel ask Samuel to appoint a king to govern them since Samuel is old and his own sons do not follow the ways of the Lord. Yet, God yearned to be Israel's only ruler and King. Jesus' mother and siblings seek to reign in his ministry, but Jesus has a larger vision and defines family as those who do the will of God. Paul reminds the church in Corinth that while our earthly bodies age and decline, our spiritual temple is being renewed daily and will last into eternity. God calls us to build things that truly last, to look beyond simple biology to find our true families, and to look beyond the outward nature of things to see God's renewal of our inner nature.

INVITATION AND GATHERING

CENTERING WORDS (2 Corinthians 5)
Should everything we cling to be destroyed, we have an imperishable house, not made with hands, but eternal in the heavens.

CALL TO WORSHIP (1 Samuel 8, Mark 3)
In this family of faith,
we have a place where we will always belong.
Here we find friends who will love us
as children of the Most High.
In this house of God,
we worship a King who rules with equity.
Here we follow One whose steadfast love
endures forever.
Whoever you are and wherever you are
on life's journey, you are welcome here.
Thanks be to God.

–OR–

CALL TO WORSHIP (Mark 3)
All who need a place to belong . . .
join the family of God.
All who seek spiritual brothers and sisters . . .
join the family of God.
All who strive to grow in faith and love . . .
join the family of God.

OPENING PRAYER (1 Samuel 8, Psalm 138, Mark 3)
Sovereign God, come to us when we lose our way.
For we need you to be our King—
    to lead us on right paths,
    teach us the ways of life and death,
      and shelter us from our foes.
We need you to be our comforter—
    to love us as a father,
    nurture us as a mother,
    shelter us as a brother,
      and assure us as a sister.
Welcome us into the arms of your mercy, O God,
    and we will be your people,
      even as you are our God and King. Amen.

PROCLAMATION AND RESPONSE

PRAYER OF YEARNING (1 Samuel 8, 2 Corinthians 4, Mark 3)
Caring Father, in the midst of our brokenness,
    knit us together as your family.
Loving Mother, in the midst of our woundedness,
    seal us in your heart as sisters and brothers.
Gentle Spirit, swing wide the doors of our church,
    that all may find within these walls
      a place where your will is done
        and holy relationships are nurtured.
In Christ's name, we pray. Amen.

WORDS OF ASSURANCE (Mark 3:34)
Christ says to us:
    "Here are my mother and my brothers.
    Whoever does the will of God
    is my brother and sister and mother."

As the family of God, we are loved and cherished
by our gracious God.

PASSING THE PEACE OF CHRIST (Mark 3)
As the family of God, let us share signs of familial love
as we pass the peace of Christ.

INTRODUCTION TO THE WORD (2 Corinthians 4:13)
Scripture proclaims: "I believed, and so I spoke." As
the words of our faith are spoken this day, listen for the
word of God.

RESPONSE TO THE WORD (Psalm 138,
1 Corinthians 4–5, Mark 3)
Even when our lives seem to be wasting away,
take heart.
God renews our inner nature.
Even when leaders fail us and our families forsake us,
take heart.
God embraces us in our family of faith.
Even when our institutions crumble
and our schedules leave us no time for rest,
take heart.
God offers us grace and mercy.

THANKSGIVING AND COMMUNION

INVITATION TO THE OFFERING (Mark 3)
As brothers and sisters of Christ, let us give joyfully
from our bounty, that all God's family may find hope
and strength through the blessings we share this day.

OFFERING PRAYER *(1 Samuel 8, Psalm 138, Mark 3)*
    Holy Sovereign, you are our King
        and we are your people.
    As we reach for our brothers and sisters in Christ,
        and our mothers and fathers in faith,
            use these offerings to heal our world
                and draw all people into your holy family.
    Amen.

SENDING FORTH

BENEDICTION *(2 Corinthians 4, Mark 3)*
    With God as our King,
    go to build God's realm here on earth.
    With our inner natures renewed,
    we go forth to proclaim God's glory.
    With your sisters and brothers in Christ
    and your mothers and fathers in faith,
    go to be Christ's family.
    With our hearts set free to love,
    we go to share Christ's love with all.

June 16, 2024

Fourth Sunday after Pentecost
Father's Day/Proper 6

Leigh Anne Taylor

COLOR

Green

SCRIPTURE READINGS

1 Samuel 15:34–16:13; Psalm 20;
2 Corinthians 5:6-10, (11-13), 14-17; Mark 4:26-34

THEME IDEAS

Today's scriptures invite us to observe the work of our Covenant God—the One who sees the king inside the child David, the greatest of all the shrubs inside the smallest of seeds, and the kingdom of God on earth as it is in heaven. The Gospel reading reminds us that the mystery of growth and transformation unfolds over time. Paul reminds us that death makes way for the birth of God's new creation for all who live for Christ. When we experience trouble along the way, the shepherd-boy-turned-king, David, invites us to place our trust in God.

INVITATION AND GATHERING

CENTERING WORDS (Mark 4)

When God sowed the seed of covenant love in Abram and Sarai, God's love extended to their whole family tree—descendants who would be more numerous than the stars in the sky. How many, like us, have found a home within its branches?

CALL TO WORSHIP (Mark 4, 2 Corinthians 5)

God of covenant love,
> **we praise you for planting seeds of your love
> within Abraham, Sarah, and their descendants.**

God of incarnate love,
> **we marvel at the magnificent family tree
> that your divine love has created among us.**

God of welcoming love,
> **we thank you that you have made a home for us
> within the branches of your family tree.**

God of everlasting love,
> **we worship you, we love you, and we honor you
> with all that we are.**

OPENING PRAYER (Mark 4)

Holy God, we humble our hearts before you
> in thanksgiving and awe.

For by your mercy, we find ourselves at home
> in the branches of your family tree.

We discover ourselves to be a people
> with a love that never fails.

We find ourselves within your grand love story
> for all time and all creation.

Whom can we thank, but you, for such great mercy?

Bring your kingdom into our midst
> as we worship you this day. Amen.

PROCLAMATION AND RESPONSE

**PRAYER OF YEARNING (1 Samuel 15–16 ,
2 Corinthians 5, Psalm 20, Mark 4)**
> Holy God, you do not see as mortals see;
>> for you look not at outward appearances
>>> but rather on the heart.
> We long to be found worthy
>> when you look upon our hearts.
> We yearn to forsake our petty grievances
>> and our unkind thoughts.
> We wish we could shuck our selfish motivations
>> and our deceptions.
> God, please help us be the best versions of ourselves.
> It's painful to admit the harm we do to one another.
> Create in our hearts a burning desire to please you.
> Grant us the courage to see our hearts as you see them,
>> and give us the wisdom to trust your love.
> For you seek to transform us into your new creations.
> Amen.

WORDS OF ASSURANCE (2 Corinthians 5, Psalm 20)
> May those who desire to please Christ,
> find the desires of their hearts.
>> **In Christ, we are a new creation.**
> Everything old has passed away.
>> **Everything has become new!**
> Glory to God!
>> **Amen.**

PASSING THE PEACE OF CHRIST (Psalm 20)
> May God grant your heart's desire! Share this hope as
> you exchange signs of Christ's peace with one another.

PRAYER OF PREPARATION (Mark 4)
Living Word of God,
like garden soil prepared for tender spring plants,
our hearts and minds are ready to receive
the gift of your divine love story.
May it live and grow in us forever. Amen.

RESPONSE TO THE WORD (2 Corinthians 5:14)
Ponder in silence what you sense the love of Christ
is urging you to do.
What would you have to say no to
to say yes to Christ's urging?
What single step toward yes
are you prepared to make today?

THANKSGIVING AND COMMUNION

INVITATION TO THE OFFERING (Psalm 20, 2 Corinthians 5)
When it comes to our resources, we build walls of security around ourselves with our money, time, energy and activity. We forget that our true home and our true security is found in God alone. May God transform our heart's desire until our actions align with God's will for our lives.

OFFERING PRAYER (Psalm 20, Mark 4)
This is our heart's desire, loving God,
that you would take our money and our time,
our prayers and our service,
and transform them into the currency
of your kingdom. Amen.

SENDING FORTH

BENEDICTION (2 Corinthians 5)
> Placing your hands over your hearts,
> > receive the new thing that God is creating
> > within you.
> Reaching your hands toward your neighbors,
> > bless the new thing that God is creating
> > within them.
> Reaching your hands toward the world,
> > bless the new thing that God is creating
> > in the world.
> **Amen!**

June 23, 2024

Fifth Sunday after Pentecost
Proper 7

Michelle L. Torigian

COLOR

Green

SCRIPTURE READINGS

1 Samuel 17:(1a, 4-11, 19-23), 32-49; Psalm 9:9-20;
2 Corinthians 6:1-13; Mark 4:35-41

THEME IDEAS

In Mark's Gospel, Jesus uses the command: "Peace! Be still" (4:39 RSV). Whether we have anxious hearts, tumultuous situations in our families, adversaries that seem to be set against us, tests of our endurance, or responsibilities to care for our neighbors, peace is craved by all.

INVITATION AND GATHERING

CENTERING PRAYER (Mark 4)
Inhale the calming presence of God, then exhale the chaos wreaking havoc on your hearts. As Christ speaks,

"Peace! Be still," feel your spirit relax and release the tempest all around.

CALL TO WORSHIP (Psalm 9)

Put your trust in God, who knows our names.
> **The Holy One does not forsake**
> **those who seek God.**

Be gracious to us, Holy One.
> **For you are the One who lifts us**
> **from the storm.**

We praise you in every time in space.
> **We rejoice that your hand guides us.**

OPENING PRAYER (Mark 4)

Holy Breath of Life, we enter this space
> searching for sacred peace.

May the winds of this hour be quiet and calming.
May the waters of this day be as peaceful as a pond.
May our hearts find the tranquility we desire.
May we fill the air with sweet songs of joy. Amen.

PROCLAMATION AND RESPONSE

PRAYER OF YEARNING (2 Corinthians 6)

Holy Generosity of Spirit,
> you are the fountain of salvation.

From your love, we see peace and comfort.
We yearn to extend the beauty of your grace
> to our neighbors,
>> instead of hoarding it for ourselves.

We long to remove the obstacles to your care
> from neighbors that need a helping hand,
>> even when it requires heavy lifting.

We seek to offer mercy to all your children,
> even when our struggles cloud our vision.

Open our hearts to the needs of our neighbors
   that we may be agents of your grace
      and messengers of your peace. Amen.

WORDS OF ASSURANCE (Mark 4, 2 Corinthians 6)
   From the great fountain of salvation,
      find peace in God's grace.
   Even amidst the hardships and storms of life,
      God's love carries us to safe harbors.
   Receive the unconditional love of God
      with hearts filled with joy.

PASSING OF THE PEACE OF CHRIST (Mark 4)
   Like Christ, who says, "Peace!" in the middle of the
   storm, may our greetings bring peace to the spirits of
   our neighbors.

RESPONSE TO THE WORD (Psalm 9)
   May the graciousness of God open our hearts.
      We place our trust in the One
      who never forsakes us.
   May peace bless and strengthen our weary hearts.
      We rest secure in the stillness of Christ.
   God's wisdom will lead us this day and always. Amen.

THANKSGIVING

INVITATION TO OFFERING (Mark 4, 2 Corinthians 6)
   God's boundless generosity transcends the limits of
   this world and nudges us to fill our land with blessing.
   Through our energy, time, talents, and treasures, we
   usher God's peace into a world filled with storms and
   obstacles.

OFFERING PRAYER (2 Corinthians 6)
> We are always rejoicing, Holy One,
>> for your many gifts in our lives.
> Even when we have nothing,
>> you make us feel as if we have everything.
> May these gifts usher peace into our world,
>> that all may know of your love
>>> and touch your grace. Amen.

SENDING FORTH

BENEDICTION (Mark 4, Psalm 9)
> May the breezes of the Spirit calm our hearts
>> as we share God's presence with the world.
> May the peace of Christ pacify our engulfed minds
>> as we go to care for our neighbors.
> The Holy One is our source of peace,
>> today and forevermore. Amen.

June 30, 2024

Sixth Sunday after Pentecost
Proper 8

Michael Beu
Copyright © Michael Beu

COLOR

Green

SCRIPTURE READINGS

2 Samuel 1:1, 17-27; Psalm 130; 2 Corinthians 8:7-15;
Mark 5:21-43

THEME IDEAS

Where do we turn in times of trial? The psalmist invites
us to wait for the Lord, more than those who wait for the
morning, for God is faithful and true. In Mark's Gospel,
both the leader of the synagogue and the woman with
the issue of blood turn to Jesus for healing. And since
the Christian community is the body of Christ, Paul invites us to turn to one another in our need. When others turn to us, Paul urges us to respond with love and
generosity. The reading from 2 Samuel does not fit this
theme but does depict a beautiful response to the death
of a loved one.

INVITATION AND GATHERING

CENTERING WORDS (Psalm 130)

Are you tossed about on the storms of life? Wait for the Lord . . . more than those who wait for the morning. Wait with hope. Wait with longing. Wait with faith.

CALL TO WORSHIP (Psalm 130)

Out of the depths, we cry to you, O Lord.
Hear our prayers and supplications.
Heed the anguish of our pleas.
Our souls wait for you alone, O Lord,
more than those who wait for the morning.
We are here to worship you this day.

OPENING PRAYER (Mark 5)

Bless and heal us, O God,
for we are stricken in body and in spirit.
As we stretch out our hands
to touch the hem of your robe,
make us well.
Course through our minds and bodies
with your healing power,
as we place our faith in your mighty Spirit,
through Jesus Christ, our Lord. Amen.

PROCLAMATION AND RESPONSE

PRAYER OF YEARNING (Psalm 130, Mark 5)

We behold those with unflinching faith, O God,
and yearn for their unquestioned assurance
of your powerful presence.

We are tired of mourning the dead
　　and long to laugh with Jairus' household
　　　　as Christ called a beloved daughter
　　　　　　back from the world beyond.
We seek not merely to be healed in body
　　but to be made whole in spirit as well.
Heal our fickle hearts as we wait for you. Amen.

WORDS OF ASSURANCE (Psalm 130)

Our Great Physician heals us, body and soul.
Give thanks to the One who answers our prayers
　　and makes us well.

PASSING THE PEACE OF CHRIST (Mark 5)

Our source of healing and peace is with us now. Let us
share this healing and peace with one another.

INTRODUCTION TO THE WORD (Philippians 1)

The One who began a good work in us leads us into holiness and righteousness. Listen well, for God is speaking still.

RESPONSE TO THE WORD or BENEDICTION (Mark 5, 2 Corinthians 8)

Bathe in the promises of God.
　　We will live as people touched by grace.
Trust the power of the One
who works in and through us.
　　We will rejoice as people touched by the Spirit.
Embrace Christ's healing, which makes us whole.
　　We will give thanks to the Lord, our God.

THANKSGIVING AND COMMUNION

INVITATION TO THE OFFERING
(2 Corinthians 8:15, CEB)

Scripture promises: *"The one who gathered more didn't have too much, and the one who gathered less didn't have too little."* May these words be fulfilled as we collect and share this morning's offering.

OFFERING PRAYER (2 Corinthians 8)

Merciful God, misery and despair
touch our world each day.
Multiply the gifts we bring before you,
that no one may suffer want.
And if our fortunes are one day reversed,
may we receive with the same grace and gratitude
we have offered this day. Amen.

SENDING FORTH

BENEDICTION (2 Corinthians 8, Mark 5)

Go in the hope and promise of God.
We will share God's love and grace.
Go in the wholeness of life with Christ.
We will share the good news of Christ's healing.
Go in the power of the Holy Spirit.
We will share the Spirit of peace with the world.

July 7, 2024

Seventh Sunday after Pentecost
Proper 9

B. J. Beu
Copyright © B. J. Beu

COLOR

Green

SCRIPTURE READINGS

2 Samuel 5:1-5, 9-10; Psalm 48; 2 Corinthians 12:2-10;
Mark 6:1-13

THEME IDEAS

What do we really need in life? Our Hebrew Scriptures
suggest we need fortified cities and a mighty warrior to
defend us. The epistle and Gospel readings, meanwhile,
suggest that true power is made perfect in weakness.
We are to take nothing for the journey as we spread the
good news and proclaim repentance in Christ's name.
If we claim to be followers of Christ, can we place our
faith in worldly might? Even when our ministries are
not received, we are to shake the dust from our sandals
and travel to those who will receive the gifts we bring in
Christ's name.

INVITATION AND GATHERING

CENTERING WORDS (Mark 6)
Take nothing for the journey of faith. Only then will we truly give God the glory for our success.

CALL TO WORSHIP (Psalm 48, 2 Corinthians 12, Mark 6)
Rely on God's providential care.
God's grace is sufficient for us.
Take nothing for the journey but faith in Christ.
We can trust the God of our salvation.
Great is the Lord and greatly to be praised.
God's steadfast love endures forever.
Come! Let us worship.

OPENING PRAYER (2 Corinthians 12, Mark 6)
Eternal Spirit, you call us to set aside our scheming
    and place our trust in you alone.
You challenge us to take nothing for the journey
    but our desire to do your will.
Teach us once more that your strength
    is made perfect in weakness,
        and that your grace is sufficient
            to meet our every need.
With the confidence of little children,
    we place our lives in your hands this day.
For we know that you will be with us
    every moment of our lives. Amen.

PROCLAMATION AND RESPONSE

PRAYER OF YEARNING (2 Corinthians 12, Mark 6)
Merciful One, we are tired in body and soul.
You teach us that your grace is sufficient,
    but we yearn for something more tangible.

You assure us that your strength
    is made perfect in weakness,
        but our weakness feels like it is killing us.
Give us humble hearts this day,
    that we may see beyond the surface
        and behold the grace you hold for us
            when we rest completely in your care.
In Christ's name, we pray. Amen.

WORDS OF ASSURANCE (2 Corinthians 12, Mark 6)

God's grace is sufficient for us
    as we take nothing for the journey
    and place our trust in God.
God's power is made perfect in weakness
    as we see beyond our limitations
    and seek to do God's will.

PASSING THE PEACE OF CHRIST (2 Corinthians 12, Mark 6)

On the road of faith, we rarely feel up to the journey. Look around at your fellow travelers, then share signs of Christ's peace, for this peace is grace and strength for the journey.

RESPONSE TO THE WORD (Psalm 48, 2 Corinthians 12, Mark 6)

God's providential care sustains us.
    God's grace meets our needs.
Christ sends us forth to share the realm of God.
    Together, we will build the kingdom of God.
The Spirit clothes us with power.
    God's steadfast love endures forever.
The Holy One leads us to life.
    Great is the Lord and greatly to be praised!

THANKSGIVING AND COMMUNION

OFFERING PRAYER (Mark 6)

You give us everything we need, O God,
    to build your kingdom.
With nothing but your presence
    and your promise to be with us,
        your presence in our lives blesses the world.
Receive our love and commitment
    in this morning's gifts and offerings,
        that the world may know
            the healing love of your Son. Amen.

SENDING FORTH

BENEDICTION (Psalm 48, Mark 6)

Go with the blessing of God, our guide and guardian.
We walk without fear to share the realm of God.
Go with the assurance of Christ, who shows us the way.
We have all we need for our journey of faith.
Go with the power of the Spirit, who anoints our way.
We travel in the footsteps of the saints of God.

July 14, 2024

Eighth Sunday after Pentecost
Proper 10

Sara Lambert

COLOR

Green

SCRIPTURE READINGS

2 Samuel 6:1-5, 12b-19; Psalm 24; Ephesians 1:3-14;
Mark 6:14-29

THEME IDEAS

The passage in 2 Samuel relates the story of King David returning the Ark of the Covenant to Jerusalem. We read of the celebration that follows, with David leading the people in dance and song. All engage in David's blessing, sharing bread, meat, and raisins. In Psalm 24, praise is given to all the earth as it belongs to the Lord, including those who live in it. We learn that those who receive the Lord's blessing must have clean hands and pure hearts. Ephesians 1 shows us that Christ claims us as his children, adopting us with redemption and forgiveness. This is our hope and joy. The passage from Mark is a challenging one, depicting the death of John the

Baptist with Herod fulfilling a promise he never antici-
pated making. Weaving these together, we find themes
of celebration, praise, and the challenges of trying to do
the right thing. Knowing that we are claimed by God—
adopted, loved, and forgiven—provides us the assurance that we belong to Christ and are strengthened
when we strive to do what's right.

INVITATION AND GATHERING

CENTERING WORDS *(2 Samuel 6, Ephesians 1)*
Dance before the Lord with instruments of praise. Know
that you are adopted into the family of God.

CALL TO WORSHIP *(2 Samuel 6, Psalm 24)*
All are welcome in the house of the Lord.
Find here the hospitality of radical fellowship.
Worship with clean hands and pure hearts.
We are lifted up by the King of glory.
We are adopted into the family of Christ.
We will leap with joy before our God!

OPENING PRAYER *(Ephesians 1, Psalm 24)*
Holy One, we enter this time of worship
with minds filled with the busyness of life.
Help us shed the dust of our toils,
relaxing in the knowledge that you claim us
just as you promised. Amen.

PROCLAMATION AND RESPONSE

PRAYER OF YEARNING *(2 Samuel 6, Ephesians 1, Mark 6)*
Lord, we come before you with open eyes
and willing hands.

Guide us as we listen for your word,
>with shouts of praise and dances of joy.
As we strive to grasp the depth of your love,
>your compassion continues to surprise and uplift us.
We yearn to be your voice in this world.
Help us discern what is right,
>as we set our hope in Christ. Amen.

WORDS OF ASSURANCE *(Ephesians 1, Psalm 24)*
Know that you are cherished
>by the good pleasure of God's love.
You are chosen by God
>and given the inheritance of Christ.
Live in truth and peace,
>and be strong in the power of the Holy Spirit.

**PASSING THE PEACE OF CHRIST *or* INTRODUCTION
TO THE WORD *(2 Samuel 6, Ephesians 1)***
May the peace of Christ fill you with the joy of God's
word.

**RESPONSE TO THE WORD *(Ephesians 1, 2 Samuel 6,
Psalm 24)***
We set our hope in Christ
>and live for the praise of his glory.
As David danced before the Lord,
>we too can offer God our thanks
>with shouts of praise and thanksgiving.

THANKSGIVING AND COMMUNION

OFFERING PRAYER *(Psalm 24, Ephesians 1, 2 Samuel 6)*
The earth is yours, O Lord, and all that is in it.
All we have comes from the richness of your grace.

As you have blessed us,
    so may we bless others.
May these offerings bind us to your love for us
    and to your love for all the world's people. Amen.

SENDING FORTH

BENEDICTION (2 Samuel 6, Ephesians 1)
    Dance before the Lord.
    Go to share God's blessings with others.
    As you journey forth,
        express Christ's love with the world.
    Go and claim the inheritance of Christ.

July 21, 2024

Ninth Sunday after Pentecost
Proper 11

B. J. Beu
Copyright © B. J. Beu

COLOR

Green

SCRIPTURE READINGS

2 Samuel 7:1-14a; Psalm 89:20-37; Ephesians 2:11-22;
Mark 6:30-34, 53-56

THEME IDEAS

God is always working to bring us peace. After defeat-
ing Israel's enemies, David is intent upon building God
a house, but God wishes David to continue his role as
shepherd, that he may bring God's people peace. True
kingship and lineage come through shepherding love
and by bringing enemies together in friendship and
kinship, not by keeping them as vassals under foot. The
peace Jesus brought, the peace attested to in both Mark
and Ephesians, is not accomplished by force of arms or
family lineage. It comes through sacrificial love—the
love of a shepherd, the love that brings reconciliation of

enemies, the love that forges strangers into a new and holy people. Ultimately, the peace that David brought through his armies could not stand, despite God's assurances that David's line would last forever. The peace Israel hoped for by vanquishing its enemies was no real peace in the end.

INVITATION AND GATHERING

CENTERING WORDS (Ephesians 2, Mark 6)
The promise of peace cannot be secured through strength of arms but through self-giving love.

CALL TO WORSHIP (Ephesians 2, Mark 6)
When you are weary in your bones . . .
here you will find rest.
When you are divided from family and friends . . .
here you will find peace.
When you are discouraged and downhearted . . .
here you will find hope and courage.
When you are looking for a shepherd to guide you . . .
here you will find succor and peace.

OPENING PRAYER (Ephesians 2, Mark 6)
Healer of division, your Son came to abolish enmity
and to create one humanity in his name.
Unite us with your saints
and bring us into the peace of your household,
that we might dwell as one family
through the one Spirit.
Be present in our worship this day
and seal us in the heart of Christ, our shepherd.
Amen.

PROCLAMATION AND RESPONSE

PRAYER OF YEARNING (Ephesians 2, Mark 6)
Shepherding God, call us away to a deserted place,
for we need your loving care.
We need your Spirit to guide us.
We need your peace to our divisions.
We yearn to abandon old grievances
and embrace wholeness in our lives.
We long to see all people,
friends and adversaries alike,
as beloved members of your household.
In this, we will find peace. Amen.

WORDS OF ASSURANCE (Ephesians 2)
As members of the household of God,
Christ calls us to be the dwelling place
for the Lord of hosts.
In Christ, we become a new humanity,
loved and made whole by the Lord of life.

PASSING THE PEACE OF CHRIST (Ephesians 2, Mark 6)
Christ's love breaks down the walls that divide us. In
joy and celebration of this great gift, let us share signs of
the peace that makes us one.

RESPONSE TO THE WORD (Psalm 89, Ephesians 2)
Like the moon in the sky, God's word endures forever.
Let the eternal word knit you together as one,
for our shepherd will heal and guide us,
as we are built into a dwelling place for God.

THANKSGIVING AND COMMUNION

INVITATION TO THE OFFERING (2 Samuel 7, Ephesians 2)
From many places and ways of life,
    God knits us together into a holy community.
From strangers, Christ builds us together
    into a holy temple in the Lord.
With thankful hearts,
    let us be generous as we collect today's offering.

OFFERING PRAYER (Ephesians 2, Mark 6)
Bringer of peace, you shaped your people
    and gave them a home.
In gratitude for your steadfast love—
    for calling us to feed in your pastures
        and rest safely in your fields—
            we bring our gifts before you this day.
May they offer the love of our shepherd
    to those in your tender care. Amen.

SENDING FORTH

BENEDICTION (Psalms 89, Ephesians 2, Mark 6)
God calls us away to bless us with rest.
    In God, we find peace.
Our shepherd watches over us day and night.
    In Christ, we dwell secure.
The Spirit anoints us with holy love.
    In the Spirit, we find healing.
Go as the beloved household of God.

July 28, 2024

Tenth Sunday after Pentecost
Proper 12

Leigh Ann Shaw

COLOR

Green

SCRIPTURE READINGS

2 Samuel 11:1-15; Psalm 14; Ephesians 3:14-21;
John 6:1-21

THEME IDEAS

The abundance of God's grace is displayed throughout
these scriptures. The challenge is to read and listen with
the eyes and ears of faith, recognizing that God goes to
profound lengths to use what is broken to bring life and
to restore what and who has meandered away. In prayer,
the Spirit and Word of God travels from our spirit to God
and from God back to our spirit. Opening to God's word
is an act of faith when we are faced with violations of
covenant or when we are challenged to trust the power
of miracles.

INVITATION AND GATHERING

CENTERING WORDS *(Ephesians 3)*

God, let the Word you have for us today fall upon our hearts and open us to your presence.

CALL TO WORSHIP *(Ephesians 3)*

May every family in heaven and on earth
gather in name and spirit.
May God pour out courage and compassion
on our congregation through the Spirit.
May our minds be open, that Christ may dwell within.
May our hearts receive the fullness of our faith.
From generation to generation,
God's grace is abundant! Amen.

OPENING PRAYER *(Ephesians 3)*

Holy Spirit, meet us here.
Find our spirits open and our hearts receptive
to your word for us this day.
With our songs and prayers,
our witness and reflection,
may we faithfully go where you call us to be.
In the name of our brother, Christ, we pray. Amen.

PROCLAMATION AND RESPONSE

PRAYER OF CONFESSION *(2 Samuel 11)*

Holy One, we come before you with contrite hearts.
You know what we've done and left undone.
You know who we've betrayed and excluded.
Yet you love us still.
We do not mean to hurt or cause harm,
yet we easily cover up our wrongs.

We bow before you in hope and trust
    that you won't push us away,
        but will draw us home once more
            into the arms of your never-failing love.
Amen.

WORDS OF ASSURANCE (2 Samuel 11)
Confessions, whether spoken aloud
or acknowledged silently within our hearts,
are pleasing to our God.
In the name of the Christ, you are forgiven.
    Thanks be to God for Christ's mercy.
    In the name of Christ, you are forgiven.

PASSING THE PEACE OF CHRIST (Ephesians 3)
Whether we come to worship with regrets and sadness or with joy and thanksgiving, passing the peace of
Christ heals the broken places in our lives and seals our
bonds of fellowship. Let us take time to share this gift of
peace with one another, both in this worship space and
in our hearts.

RESPONSE TO THE WORD (Ephesians 3)
This is the living Word of God,
lifted before the people of God.
    We kneel in heart with gratitude
    for God's unfailing Word. Amen.

THANKSGIVING AND COMMUNION

INVITATION TO THE OFFERING (Ephesians 3)
God's grace is abundant. Wherever we wander, God
remains our God. The profoundness of God's love
stands in contrast to the harsh judgment of our world.
In response to this unfailing love, let us bring our time,

161

talents, and treasures to serve the ministries to which we are called.

OFFERING PRAYER (*Ephesians 3*)
>Merciful Lord, there is nowhere we can go—
>>in the heavens above,
>>>or the earth and ocean below—
>>>>to escape your loving care.
>Receive today the offering we make
>>and bless our gifts,
>>>that they may be a blessing.
>May this offering reflect our sincerest hope
>>that all may be filled with your fullness.
>In the name of the one who calls us, we pray. Amen.

SENDING FORTH

BENEDICTION (*2 Samuel 11*)
>Despite our failure, God redeems us
>>and gives us a name.
>We belong to God.
>Go forth into the world, assured and confident
>>that you are claimed by the One who gives life.
>With all you do, share this grace with all you meet.
>In all you do, represent Christ's magnificent love.
>Amen.

August 4, 2024

Eleventh Sunday after Pentecost
Proper 13

James Dollins

COLOR

Green

SCRIPTURE READINGS

2 Samuel 11:26–12:13a; Psalm 51:1-12; Ephesians 4:1-16;
John 6:24-35

THEME IDEAS

More and more, we find ourselves spiritually hungry.
Increasingly, we are isolated and deprived of the love
we need. In John's Gospel, Jesus offers the bread of life
to satisfy us, that we may never hunger or thirst again.
Paul's letter to the Ephesians calls us to be one with one
another, speak the truth in love, and equip God's saints
for ministry. Let us no longer deny ourselves or others
the spiritual food we need. May we feast together on the
bread Christ offers us.

INVITATION AND GATHERING

CENTERING WORDS (John 6)
Are you spiritually well-fed? Eat well of the bread of life. Drink your fill of the living water, and share this feast with every hungry guest.

CALL TO WORSHIP (John 6)
We do not live by bread alone,
but by the life-giving word of God's love.
God, give us the bread of life,
today and always.
Too long have we lived with hunger,
seeking to fill our appetites with food
that leaves us wanting.
Too long we have starved ourselves
of spiritual food that truly satisfies.
"I am the Bread of Life," Jesus tells us.
"Whoever comes to me will never be hungry."
"Whoever believes in me will never be thirsty."
Come, Holy Spirit. Feed us with your grace and love.
May we love our neighbors, ourselves, and you,
so that we may never be hungry again. Amen.

OPENING PRAYER (John 6)
Spirit of God, dwell among us and revive us.
You know the deep hungers that motivate us,
and the attempts we make to satisfy these hungers.
You alone know the grace and peace
that can nourish us to full strength, in body and soul.
Feed us, Bread of Life, with food that lasts.
Give enough to share with others who also hunger,
even if they know not what they hunger for.
We rejoice in your bread,
for it truly satisfies.

Give us the wisdom to receive it,
that we may taste and see your goodness, O Lord.
Amen.

PROCLAMATION AND RESPONSE

PRAYER OF YEARNING (John 6, Ephesians 4)

God of abundance, you long to feed your children,
whenever we are hungry.
Yet we often turn away
and seek happiness elsewhere.
When we compete with others for status,
help us support one another in love.
When we measure our worth by our productivity,
help us rest in the assurance
that we are your children.
When we avoid conflict,
move us to speak your truth in love.
Return us to your ways, Holy One,
that our souls may be satisfied
and our hearts may be at peace. Amen.

WORDS OF ASSURANCE or INVITATION TO COMMUNION (John 6)

Christ's table is open to all who will join the feast.
Come, eat; be loved and forgiven.
Then share this good food with all who hunger.
Glory be to God. Amen.

RESPONSE TO THE WORD (John 6)

People of God, let us receive the grace of God.
**We will practice self-compassion,
feeding our souls with good food.**
People of God, let us learn to love one another.
**We will generously love family, friends,
and our neighbors.**

People of God, love God with all your heart.
Christ, the bread of life, longs for us
to feast with God and with one another.
People of God, hunger and thirst for justice.
We cannot be satisfied until all of God's children
join the table.
Be hungry no longer; receive what God has offered.
Fill us, Holy Spirit, with the grace we crave,
that we may hunger and thirst no more. Amen.

THANKSGIVING AND COMMUNION

OFFERING PRAYER (John 6, Ephesians 4)
Generous God, you have fed us well
    in body and in spirit.
Your grace never runs short,
    but meets us in our need.
Make us one with all your children,
    that these gifts and our good works
        may bring comfort to those who grieve,
            friendship to those who are lonely,
                and provision to those who are in need.
This we pray, in your blessed name. Amen.

SENDING FORTH

BENEDICTION (John 6)
Stay well-nourished by God's grace
    and share the bread of life with others.
May the grace of Christ, the love of God,
    and the communion of the Holy Spirit,
    be with us now and forevermore. Amen.

August 11, 2024

Twelfth Sunday after Pentecost
Proper 14

Karin Ellis

COLOR

Green

SCRIPTURE READINGS

2 Samuel 18:5-9, 15, 31-33; Psalm 130;
Ephesians 4:25–5:2; John 6:35, 41-51

THEME IDEAS

Themes of life and death fill today's scriptures. We encounter a grieving parent in 2 Samuel, as David mourns the loss of his son, Absalom. The psalmist echoes the grief we feel when we cry out from the depths to God, who will bring forgiveness, redemption, and hope. From death to life, Paul reminds the Ephesians to live in community, as they strive to be imitators of Christ. And Jesus, the one who brings new life, reveals that he is the bread of life; he is all we need. May we pay attention to the moments of life and death in our lives, and remember that God is with us through it all.

INVITATION AND GATHERING

CENTERING WORDS (2 Samuel 18, Ephesians 4)
Bring your whole heart before God—all your grief, anger, frustration, joy, hope, and praise. God loves and welcomes you just as you are!

CALL TO WORSHIP (Psalm 130)
We have gathered from different places
and different backgrounds.
May those who are grieving find comfort.
May those who have turned away from God
find forgiveness.
May those who are waiting find hope.
May all find God's steadfast love and grace.
Let us worship the One who gives us life!

OPENING PRAYER (Ephesians 4, John 6)
Jesus, bread of life, you give us life
and nourish our spirits.
As your beloved children,
help us walk in your ways, each and every day.
May we speak words of kindness to one another
and open our hearts to share comfort
and encouragement.
May we offer and seek forgiveness.
Most of all, may we remember that your steadfast love
extends to all of your beloved children.
In your holy name, we pray. Amen.

PROCLAMATION AND RESPONSE

PRAYER OF YEARNING (Psalm 130, Ephesians 4)
O Lord, we cry out to you!
We cry out for help:
    when we turn away from you;
    when we ignore the needs of our neighbors;
    when we speak harsh words to those around us;
    when we forget that we are your beloved children.
Draw us close and embrace us with your steadfast love
    and your healing grace.
In your merciful name, we pray. Amen.

WORDS OF ASSURANCE (Psalm 130, John 6)
Beloved children of God, the Lord offers wholeness
    and new life to those who seek it.
In the name of Christ, you are one with God!
Thanks be to God! Amen.

PASSING THE PEACE OF CHRIST
Jesus says, "I am the bread of life." In the name of Christ,
I invite you to share the peace of Christ, the one who
brings new life and nourishment to our souls.

PRAYER OF PREPARATION (Ephesians 4)
May the words that are spoken build up this community.
May the ears that hear receive the good news
    of God's grace.
And may the Holy Spirit move us to action,
    so that our community may be filled
        with love and healing. Amen.

RESPONSE TO THE WORD *(Psalm 130 and John 6)*
We have heard words of hope and new life.
May these words help us live in the ways of God:
ways of comfort and peace,
ways of steadfast love and mercy.
Praise be to God!

THANKSGIVING

INVITATION TO THE OFFERING *(2 Samuel 18; Ephesians 4)*
God is here, welcoming us just as we are.
In thanksgiving for all God has blessed us with,
and in gratitude for all the ways God loves us,
may we bring our offerings before God.

OFFERING PRAYER *(2 Samuel 18; Ephesians 4)*
Gracious God, we bring these gifts to you,
that you may bless them.
May they bring comfort to those who mourn,
help to those in need,
and joy to all your beloved children. Amen.

SENDING FORTH

BENEDICTION *(2 Samuel 18, Ephesians 4, John 6)*
Brothers and sisters, siblings in Christ,
may you find comfort in God's grace.
May you find strength in Christ's love.
And may you find encouragement in the Spirit's power.
Go in peace. Amen.

August 18, 2024

Thirteenth Sunday after Pentecost
Proper 15

Michael Beu
Copyright © Michael Beu

COLOR

Green

SCRIPTURE READINGS

1 Kings 2:10-12; 3:3-14; Psalm 111; Ephesians 5:15-20;
John 6:51-58

THEME IDEAS

Wisdom and the benefits of wise behavior focus today's readings. In 1 Kings, Solomon inherits the throne of his father David. Yet, rather than asking God for selfish gain, Solomon asks for the understanding and wisdom to lead God's people. The psalmist suggests that wisdom begins with awe and reverence for God: "Fear of the LORD is where wisdom begins" (v. 10 CEB). The epistle advocates wisdom, warning against foolish behavior. And in John's Gospel, Jesus proclaims the wisdom of partaking of his body and blood to attain eternal life.

INVITATION AND GATHERING

CENTERING WORDS (1 Kings 2)

A discerning mind is more to be desired than great wealth or long life. A heart that distinguishes good from evil is more to be sought than earthly power and prestige.

CALL TO WORSHIP (1 Kings 2, Ephesians 5)

Rejoice, seekers of wisdom and truth,
> **God's wisdom calls us here.**

Behold, followers of godly direction and guidance,
> **Christ's love shows us the way.**

Sing, children of thanksgiving and praise,
> **the Spirit's presence gathers us together.**

OPENING PRAYER (1 Kings 2)

God of steadfast love,
> you granted young Solomon
>> the wisdom to rule your people with judgment
>> and understanding.

When we turn to you for answers,
> you grant us the wisdom to discern good and evil
> and bestow the courage to live in your ways.

Be with us in this time of worship,
> as we seek to grow in your wisdom
> and abide in your grace. Amen.

PROCLAMATION AND RESPONSE

PRAYER OF YEARNING (Ephesians 5, John 6)

Source of wisdom and understanding,
> turn us from the folly that surrounds us
> as we seek to live according to your ways.

Fill us with your Spirit of power,
and guard us from the selfish paths
that blind us to your call
to seek justice and mercy.
Bless us with your Spirit once more,
that we may follow in the footsteps of your Son
and live in your holy ways. Amen.

WORDS OF ASSURANCE (John 6)

Ask and you shall receive.
Seek and you shall find.
For the Lord is full of wisdom and grace,
offering new life in Christ.

PASSING THE PEACE OF CHRIST (1 Kings 2, Ephesians 5)

As we seek God's wisdom and guidance, let us share signs of fellowship and peace with one another this day.

RESPONSE TO THE WORD (Mark 5, 2 Corinthians 8)

Wisdom is a gift from God.
God, grant us wisdom.
Understanding flows from the heart of Christ.
Christ, grant us understanding.
Life is a blessing from the Spirit.
Holy Spirit, grant us life eternal.

THANKSGIVING AND COMMUNION

INVITATION TO THE OFFERING (Psalm 111)

We see God's work in acts of honesty and justice. We touch God's covenant in moments of mercy and compassion. Let us be God's instruments in the world, as we collect today's offering.

OFFERING PRAYER (Psalm 111, John 6)
God of wisdom and understanding,
　　your blessings surround us each day.
We thank you for inspiring our actions
　　and feeding our creativity.
We praise you for warming our hearts
　　and enlightening our minds.
May these gifts go forth into your world
　　and be bread and blessing to those in need. Amen.

INVITATION TO COMMUNION (John 6)
The bread of heaven enlivens our souls.
　　We draw strength from the bread of life.
The cup of blessing brings saving grace.
　　We find life in the cup of salvation.
Eat and drink, for all are welcome here.
　　Taste the goodness of God's heavenly banquet.

COMMUNION PRAYER (John 6)
Lord of life, you are the living bread
　　that came down from heaven.
Give us this bread,
　　that we may never hunger.
Source of promise, you are the cup of salvation
　　that was poured out for many.
Give us this cup of blessing,
　　that we may never thirst. Amen.

SENDING FORTH

BENEDICTION (1 Kings 2, Psalm 111, Ephesians 5)
God sends us forth with wisdom and understanding.
　　We go to be a blessing to the world.
God sends us forth to be honest and just.
　　We go to be a blessing to the world.
Go with God.

August 25, 2024

Fourteenth Sunday after Pentecost
Proper 16

Mary Scifres
Copyright © Mary Scifres

COLOR

Green

SCRIPTURE READINGS

1 Kings 8:(1, 6, 10-11), 22-30, 41-43; Psalm 84;
Ephesians 6:10-20; John 6:56-69

THEME IDEAS

God's sustenance and strength come in many forms—
in glorious places of worship and meaningful rituals; in
protective power and faithful love; in words of encouragement and challenge; and, most beautifully, in Christ
Jesus, who is the bread of life and the bread of our lives.

INVITATION AND GATHERING

CENTERING WORDS

God's light is shining. Christ's love is flowing. The Spirit's presence is here, sustaining and strengthening us.

CALL TO WORSHIP (1 Kings 8, Psalm 84, Ephesians 6)
God is our sun and our shield.
God's glory shines upon us.
God is our strength and our hope.
God's faithfulness guides us.
God is our hope and our salvation.
God's love and mercy welcome us.

OPENING PRAYER (1 Kings 8, Ephesians 6)
God of grace and glory,
pour out the power of your Holy Spirit
on our worship and our gathering.
Strengthen and protect us
with your steadfast faithfulness.
Feed us with the bread of life,
and guide our steps with the wisdom of your word.
In your holy name, we pray. Amen.

PROCLAMATION AND RESPONSE

PRAYER OF YEARNING (1 Kings 8, Ephesians 6)
Glorious God of spirit and life,
we long to look upon your face and live.
We yearn to shine with your glory,
despite our tarnished lives.
We seek to stand firm and faithful,
even when the storms of life threaten us.
Lift us up with your mercy,
that we may perceive your loving grace.
Light our paths with your wisdom
and strengthen us with your powerful Spirit,
that we may follow you faithfully
all the days of our lives. Amen.

WORDS OF ASSURANCE (Psalm 84, Ephesians 6, John 6)
God is our sun and our shield.
Christ is the bread of our lives.
The Spirit is our strength and our power.
In these truths, we are clothed with protection
    to live with justice, truth, and peace.

PASSING THE PEACE OF CHRIST (Ephesians 6)
Clothed with the peace of God, led by the Prince of
peace, strengthened by the Spirit of peace, share signs
of peace and love with one another and with those we
meet in the days ahead.
*(Encourage online worshipers to share comments of peace and
joy on your video platform. If appropriate, invite all worshipers to take a moment to send a text message of joy and love to
someone who isn't in worship today.)*

INTRODUCTION TO THE WORD (John 6)
Listen, even if the words seem harsh.
Listen, even if the lessons seem hard.
Listen, even if you've heard it before.
Listen, even if it's something you may already know.
For in the listening, the Spirit speaks wisdom
    to our hearts.
This wisdom is beyond mere hearing—
    it is wisdom from above.

RESPONSE TO THE WORD (Ephesians 6, John 6)
Do you feel weak and defenseless?
    Are you asking if we are strong?
Do you want to leave, as some disciples did?
    Are you asking if we are able?
These are the questions I ask myself.
    We will stand firm and follow faithfully,
    for Christ leads the way.

May these words of hope be shields and protection.
**May these words of hope be spirit and truth
for our lives.**

THANKSGIVING AND COMMUNION

INVITATION TO THE OFFERING (1 Kings 8, John 6)
As God has welcomed us, so God invites us to welcome
others with generous gifts and heartfelt love. May we
share our offerings and gifts in this spirit of generosity
and love.

OFFERING PRAYER (John 6)
Bread of heaven, thank you for nourishing us
with your mercy and your grace.
Thank you for blessing us to be your disciples—
disciples who share freely with your world.
May our gifts and offerings
become food and blessings for your world. Amen.

SENDING FORTH

BENEDICTION (Ephesians 6)
Led by Christ,
we go now to serve.
Strengthened by the Spirit,
we go to bring justice and peace.
Guided by God,
we go in God's glory and grace. Amen.

September 1, 2024

Fifteenth Sunday after Pentecost
Proper 17

Rebecca J. Gaudino

COLOR

Green

SCRIPTURE READINGS

Song of Solomon 2:8-13; Psalm 45:1-2, 6-9; James 1:17-27; Mark 7:1-8, 14-15, 21-23

THEME IDEAS

James sketches out a cycle in the gospel ecosystem using creation language. Coming down from God, "the creator of the heavenly lights," is "every good gift, every perfect gift" (James 1:17, CEB). This downpouring is also the new birth that God gives us through the word of truth "planted deep inside you—the very word that is able to save you" (1:21). What does this downpouring bring forth? James writes that the newly born are like a "first crop from the harvest of everything" God has created (1:18). We are fruit and grain for the world, care for the orphan and widow. God's good gifts to us become our good gifts to others. In both James and Mark, Jesus warns us about other "crops" that grow within us and in our midst—anger, pride, envy, greed, and so on. But these do not complete the cycle. Jesus provides the last hoped-for step of the gospel eco-cycle: honor rising to God as we live into the people God created us to be (Mark 7:6-7).

INVITATION AND GATHERING

CENTERING WORDS (Mark 7)
My heart longs to be close to you, O God.
May my life and my deeds honor you.

CALL TO WORSHIP (James 1, Mark 7)
Creator, you bless us with the heavenly lights—
the moon that waxes and wanes,
the planets that whirl around the sun,
the galaxies that wink from afar.
In the darkness you call out, "Let there be light,"
and the universe is filled with heavenly light.
You are our creator, too,
the One who formed us and who forms us still.
May your word of truth ring out today
with your call to new life!
Amen.

OPENING PRAYER (James 1, Mark 7)
Creator of the heavenly lights,
there is no shadow in your divine light.
It remains unchanging across the eons,
even as the stars come and go.
You are our faithful creator,
the Gardener of our lives.
You plant your truth within us
and inspire lives of caring and love.
We honor and worship you. Amen.

PROCLAMATION AND RESPONSE

PRAYER OF YEARNING (James 1, Mark 7)

Ever-faithful God, you create each of us
    to be a presence of healing and love in our world.
You equip us to resist intentions and actions
    that hurt ourselves and others.
Forgive us when we forget your desire for us.
Forgive us when we put aside your vision.
Remind us of the love and goodness
    that you have planted within us.
Draw our hearts close to you
    and bless us as we live in your ways. Amen.

WORDS OF ASSURANCE (James 1)

God has chosen to give us new life.
This is God's choice, given freely to us,
    as is every other good gift God has given.
Rejoice in this good news!

PRAYER OF PREPARATION (James 1)

God of the gardens, you plan a bountiful harvest
    from the crop of our lives.
Plant your seeds of truth in the soil of who we are
    and what we do. Amen.

RESPONSE TO THE WORD (James 1, Mark 7)

May our hearts draw close to you, Giver of new birth.
May we honor you with our lives, Divine Gardener.
May we hear and do your word of truth. Amen.

THANKSGIVING AND COMMUNION

INVITATION TO THE OFFERING (James 1)

God calls us to a devotion that is pure and faultless.
What does such devotion look like? Caring for those in
a world with big needs and little hope. Let us give as
generously as God has given to us.

OFFERING PRAYER (James 1, Mark 7)

God of every good gift,
    bless the gifts of our resources,
        our prayers, and our lives.
Bless these gifts for the good of others
    and to the honor of your name. Amen.

SENDING FORTH

BENEDICTION (James 1, Mark 7)

The good gifts of God continue to pour out upon us,
giving us inspiration and energy for every good act.
    **May our lives yield a full harvest of goodness
    and compassion!**
Go and be doers of God's word of truth!
    May our lives honor God! Amen.

September 8, 2024

Sixteenth Sunday after Pentecost
Proper 18

Mary Scifres
Copyright © Mary Scifres

COLOR

Green

SCRIPTURE READINGS

Proverbs 22:1-2, 8-9, 22-23; Psalm 125; James 2:1-10, (11-13), 14-17; Mark 7:24-37

THEME IDEAS

Everyone matters to God, so everyone should matter to us. Today's readings, even with their different messages, warn that favoritism and prejudice blind us to the truth that everyone matters equally to God. When we favor the rich over the poor, or the familiar and included over the unfamiliar and excluded, we limit our ability to live faithfully as followers of God. Even Jesus had to learn this lesson, so it's no wonder scripture guides us to do the same.

INVITATION AND GATHERING

CENTERING WORDS *(James 2, Mark 7)*
Everyone matters or no one matters. Here, everyone matters, and all are welcomed by the love of God.

CALL TO WORSHIP *(James 2, Mark 7)*
Place your trust in God.
God's faithfulness is unshakeable.
May our worship this day strengthen our faith.
May our faithfulness be unshakeable.
May our words and actions be good and true.
May we grow in godliness each and every day.

OPENING PRAYER *(James 2, Mark 7)*
We place our trust in you, O God,
for your love and faithfulness are steadfast and true.
Breathe your Holy Spirit into our worship
and your very presence into our lives,
that our love and faithfulness
may be steadfast and true. Amen.

PROCLAMATION AND RESPONSE

PRAYER OF YEARNING *(Proverbs 22, James 2, Mark 7)*
Creator God, you create all people in your image.
When we neglect the needs of the poor,
raise our commitment to care for others
and to help create justice for all.
When favoritism and prejudice blind us,
and when we exclude and demean others,
focus us on your inclusive love,
a love that welcomes us
and calls us to welcome others.

Live in us and through us,
  that our lives and our actions
    may reflect your image
      in all that we say and in all that we do.
Amen.

WORDS OF ASSURANCE (Psalm 125, James 2)
God is good
  all the time.
And all the time,
  God is good.
In God's goodness, we touch goodness.
  In God's love, we receive love.
In God's grace and mercy,
  we find fellowship with God's people.

PASSING THE PEACE OF CHRIST
As forgiven and reconciled children of Christ, let's share signs of reconciliation, love, and welcome with one another.

INTRODUCTION TO THE WORD (Proverbs 22, James 2)
Listen, dear brothers and sisters, for God's wisdom meets us here.

RESPONSE TO THE WORD (James 2, Mark 7)
Sisters and brothers, what good is faith
if we do nothing with it?
  Our faith is shown by our actions.
May we have a living faith,
a faith that brings life and hope to God's creation.
  May our words and our actions reflect the love,
  that God places within us.
They will know we are Christians by our love,
  a love shown through good works.

THANKSGIVING AND COMMUNION

INVITATION TO THE OFFERING (Proverbs 22, James 2, Mark 7)

God has chosen the poor as heirs of God's kingdom. God calls us to value the needs of this world more highly than we value silver and gold. May our offerings reflect the values to which God calls us.

OFFERING PRAYER (James 2, Mark 7)

Through these gifts and offerings,
bless your world, O God.
Through our lives and our actions,
bring love to your creation,
that all may know your presence
and live in your grace. Amen.

SENDING FORTH

BENEDICTION (James 2, Mark 7)

Go as God's children.
We go as Christ's hands and feet.
Go as God's faithful followers.
We go to live our faith with love in action.

September 15, 2024

Seventeenth Sunday after Pentecost
Proper 19

Kirsten Linford

COLOR

Green

SCRIPTURE READINGS

Proverbs 1:20-33; Psalm 19; James 3:1-12; Mark 8:27-38

THEME IDEAS

The crux of these texts lies with the question of when to speak and when to keep silent, while encouraging us to continue listening and learning. In Proverbs, Wisdom calls to us; we ignore her at our peril. The author of James reminds us that those who teach are held to a higher standard and that it's as important to determine when to keep silent as it is to know when to speak. In the Gospel passage, Jesus is adamant about speaking the truth of his death and resurrection, even as he exhorts the disiciples to refrain from speaking his name to others or registering their discomfort with his truth. The psalmist encourages us to speak of God's glory and wisdom as eloquently as the heavens do.

INVITATION AND GATHERING

CENTERING WORDS *(Proverbs 1, Psalm 19)*

The heavens are telling the glory of God. The firmament proclaims God's handiwork. What wisdom do we hear? What wisdom do we share?

CALL TO WORSHIP *(Psalm 19)*

The heavens are telling the glory of God.
>   **The firmament proclaims God's handiwork.**
Day pours forth speech,
>   **and night declares knowledge of our God.**
God's wisdom is written in the stars.
>   **It is seen and heard to the ends of the earth.**
When we see God's teachings in the clouds,
>   **or hear them in the symphonies of the birds,**
our minds are enriched,
>   **our eyes are enlightened,**
our souls are revived,
>   **and our hearts rejoice.**
Then we shall bless God's name with our words,
>   **and with the silence between them.**

OPENING PRAYER *(Proverbs 1)*

O God, your Wisdom speaks in our streets,
>   cries out from our intersections,
>>   and calls our names.
Wisdom hopes we will stop . . . listen . . . and learn.
Wisdom beseeches us to turn our faces
>   and our ears to you.
Wisdom urges us to bless your name
>   with our speaking . . . and our silence.
May we speak and bless your name, O God,
>   now and always. Amen.

PROCLAMATION AND RESPONSE

PRAYER OF YEARNING (James 3)
> O God, we long for you—
>> for your love,
>> for your wisdom,
>> for your grace.
>
> We long for the words of your mouth,
>> when we cannot find our own.
>
> We long for the courage to speak
>> and sing your blessings.
>
> We pray for the wisdom to keep silent,
>> rather than speak words of harm.
>
> Be our vision, O God, and our voice.
> And may our mouths proclaim your praise. Amen.

WORDS OF ASSURANCE (Mark 8)
> When we are too afraid to speak the truth,
>> Christ will speak it with us
>> and even through us,
>> until it is heard and known.
>
> Even when we lose ourselves or our way,
>> Christ will give it back to us,
>> saving us again and again. Amen.

PASSING THE PEACE OF CHRIST (James 3)
> The Holy One has given us mouths to praise God and tongues to bless God's people, our siblings in faith. Let us turn and share God's grace and peace with one another this day.

PRAYER OF PREPARATION (Psalm 19)
> May the words of my mouth . . .
>> **and the meditations of our hearts**
>> **be acceptable in your sight, O Lord,**
>>> **our strength and our redeemer. Amen.**

RESPONSE TO THE WORD (Psalm 19)
  The Word of God is a blessing to us—
      enriching our minds,
      enlightening our eyes,
      rejoicing our hearts,
          and reviving our souls.
  The Word of God is more precious than gold.
  We have heard the Word.
  Now may it work within us and through us
      to bring wisdom and eternal life. Amen.

THANKSGIVING AND COMMUNION

INVITATION TO THE OFFERING (Proverbs 1)
  God's gifts of wisdom are offered in this moment and in
  every moment. In gratitude and grace, let us offer our
  gifts to God.

OFFERING PRAYER (Proverbs 1, Psalm 19, James 3, Mark 8)
  For your holy Word, O God,
      we give you thanks.
  For your enduring Wisdom, O God,
      we give you praise.
  For your call to speak truth, O God,
      we give you glory.
  Grant us the courage to share your gifts,
      this day and all days. Amen.

SENDING FORTH

BENEDICTION (James 3)
  People of God, go into the world
      and speak God's blessing and God's grace
      in word and action. Amen.

September 22, 2024

Eighteenth Sunday after Pentecost
Proper 20

Michelle Torigian

COLOR

Green

SCRIPTURE READINGS

Proverbs 31:10-31; Psalm 1; James 3:13–4:3, 7-8a;
Mark 9:30-37

THEME IDEAS

What does it mean to be righteous? According to Jesus,
it is to be humble and to welcome the marginalized.
According to James, the righteous one grasps wisdom
from God instead of living a life filled with "bitter jealousy and selfish ambition" (James 3:14 CEB). According to the psalmist, this righteousness and a focus on
God's law bring happiness. Strength and kindness lead
the wife in Proverbs 31 to a life of righteousness and
courage.

INVITATION AND GATHERING

CENTERING PRAYER *(James 3, Proverbs 31, Mark 9)*
Breathe in and invite the Spirit of Wisdom to fill your soul. Breathe out, recalling the Spirit of Love that connects you with all God's children.

CALL TO WORSHIP *(Proverbs 31, Psalm 1, James 3)*
Happy are those who follow paths of righteousness.
We take delight in the wisdom of God.
Happy are those who reach out to those in need.
We find delight in the love of God.
Happy are those who set aside envy.
We draw delight in the selflessness of God.

OPENING PRAYER *(Psalm 1, James 3)*
Holy Stream of Righteousness—
   as we embrace the dawn of this week
     and the reemergence of hope in our lives,
      we sing your praises.
As we face the journey before us,
   we seek your wisdom and your strength.
Erase the envy from our minds
   and the biases from our hearts,
     as we enter this space.
Fill our lives with the refreshing brooks
   of your peace. Amen.

PROCLAMATION AND RESPONSE

PRAYER OF CONFESSION *(Proverbs 31, James 3)*
Divine Source of Understanding,
   discord rages in the airwaves around us,
     leading us to challenge your holy wisdom.

Confusion swirls within our daily lives,
    contributing to the discord in our world.
Our selfish desires consume our attention,
    blocking your voice and the needs of others
        from our view.
May your peace still the whirlwind within our minds
    and help us hear your holy wisdom
        as we walk our journey of faith.
And may kindness spring forth from our tongues,
    each and every day. Amen.

WORDS OF ASSURANCE (Psalm 1)

The Grace of God can transform our hearts,
    even amidst a cacophony of noise.
The wisdom of God beckons to our souls,
    revealing our world in a different light.
In due season, we will yield the fruit of faith
    in our adventure with God.

PASSING OF THE PEACE OF CHRIST (Mark 9)

In a spirit of humility, recognize the ways we are called
to grow with God and neighbor. May we greet one another as God's children with the peace of Christ.

RESPONSE TO THE WORD (Psalm 31)

As the Spirit works with our hearts,
    may our works be as precious as jewels.
As the Spirit nudges us to embrace holy wisdom,
    may we gird ourselves with strength.
As the Spirit sets kindness upon our tongues,
    may we meet the needs of our neighbors.

THANKSGIVING

INVITATION TO OFFERING (Proverbs 31, Mark 9)
The righteousness of God sets aside bias and jealousy as we welcome the opportunity to care for God's children. Listen to the winds of hope. Look for the light of wisdom. May this light remain steadfast as we seek ways to share our treasures, talents, and time.

OFFERING PRAYER (Proverbs 31, Mark 9, James 3)
Beloved One, with the work of our hands,
    we create pathways of care.
With open hearts, we welcome your abundant wisdom
    which invites us to share.
May our gifts transform our communities
    into places of humility and generosity. Amen.

SENDING FORTH

BENEDICTION (Proverbs 31, Psalm 1, James 3, Mark 9)
May divine strength be our clothing.
May holy righteousness be our guide.
May the wisdom of God usher us on our path.
May the Love of Christ yield fields of mercy.
May we delight in our adventures with God,
    each moment of our lives. Amen.

September 29, 2024

Nineteenth Sunday after Pentecost
Proper 21

Mary Scifres
Copyright © Mary Scifres

COLOR

Green

SCRIPTURE READINGS

Esther 7:1-6, 9-10; 9:20-22; Psalm 124; James 5:13-20;
Mark 9:38-50

THEME IDEAS

The power of community emerges in today's scriptures. Esther works within the palace community to save her people, who are largely outside of the palace community. James reminds us that praying with and for one another is a game changer in the life of faith. And Jesus reminds his followers that even their community will be strengthened by outsiders who claim the name of Jesus and who perform acts of compassion and healing. Ultimately, the power of community can lead us to either hurt or heal. The challenge is to create a path of peace, love and justice, while also inviting and welcoming others onto path with us.

INVITATION AND GATHERING

CENTERING WORDS *(James 5, Mark 9)*
Salt the world with peace and flavor the world with love.

CALL TO WORSHIP *(James 5, Mark 9)*
We gather to pray.
We gather to praise.
May our prayers extend beyond ourselves.
May our praise rise to the heavens.
May our lives be salty with love.
May our prayers be reflections of peace.

OPENING PRAYER *(James 5, Mark 9, Esther 7)*
Faithful God, inspire us to be faithful to one another.
Open our hearts to meet the needs in our midst
and in the wider world.
Open our minds to notice the beauty and gift
of your creation.
Open our mouths to sing your blessings,
joyfully and gratefully.
Open our lives to welcome the stranger, seek the lost,
and create peace in a troubled world. Amen.

PROCLAMATION AND RESPONSE

PRAYER OF YEARNING *(James 5, Mark 9, Esther 7)*
O God, you are our help and our hope.
In times of trial,
keep us from falling into temptation.
In times of need,
help us reach out for aid and lean on prayer.
Show us that others need our help, our hope,
and our prayers.

Strengthen our resolve to offer those gifts
    where they are most needed.
When we become lost,
        welcome us home with mercy and grace,
            that we may do the same for others.
In hope and gratitude, we pray. Amen.

WORDS OF ASSURANCE (Psalm 124, James 5)
The Lord is for us, our help and our hope.
In God's mercy and grace,
        we are welcomed with love
        and forgiven with compassion.
Thanks be to God for helping us along the way.

PASSING THE PEACE OF CHRIST (Mark 9)
God has flavored our lives with mercy and love. May
we flavor this community with these gifts as we share
signs of Christ's peace with one another.

**RESPONSE TO THE WORD or PRAYER OF
INTERCESSION AND THANKS (James 5)**
We know there is suffering in our midst.
    We pray with and for one another.
We know there is illness in our midst.
    We pray with and for one another.
Gracious God, hear us as we pray for those
who are suffering in body, mind, and soul.
(Moment of silent prayer or lifting of names and needs)
We know there is joy in our midst.
    We praise God with and for one another.
We know there are blessings in our midst.
    We praise God with and for one another.
*(Moment of silent prayer or the lifting of names, joys, and
blessings)*
In trust and thanksgiving, we pray.
    Amen.

THANKSGIVING AND COMMUNION

INVITATION TO THE OFFERING (James 5, Mark 9)

As we have offered our prayers and our praise to God,
now may we offer our gifts and our tithes for a world in
need of our church and our ministry.

OFFERING PRAYER (James 5, Mark 9)

As you have blessed us, gracious God,
bless the gifts we return to you now.
May our tithes and offerings
bless your world with love
and salt your world with peace. Amen.

SENDING FORTH

BENEDICTION (Psalm 124, Mark 9)

Our help is in the name of God,
maker of heaven and earth.
Our help leads us forth
to bring peace and love to the earth.
Our help goes with us
to protect us and to guide our way.
Amen.
And amen.

October 6, 2024

Twentieth Sunday after Pentecost
World Communion Sunday
Proper 22

Hans Holznagel

COLOR

Green

SCRIPTURE READINGS

Job 1:1; 2:1-10; Psalm 26; Hebrews 1:1-4; 2:5-12;
Mark 10:2-16

THEME IDEAS

Suffering is present all over the world. God knows
it and is not indifferent. Characters in today's texts
range from heavenly angels to Satan, and from Job, the
long-sufferer, to Jesus, the eternal Word and "pioneer
of salvation," whose solidarity with humanity comes,
in part, because he too knows suffering.

INVITATION AND GATHERING

CENTERING WORDS (*Hebrews 2:6, NRSVUE*)
"What are humans that you are mindful of them or mortals that you care for them?" Not angels, to be sure. Just people, the beloved children of God.

CALL TO WORSHIP (*Job 2, Psalm 26*)
Your steadfast love is before our eyes, O God.
Help us move in faithfulness.
When tests and trials come—when evil itself appears—
we place our trust in you, O Knower of joy and suffering.
Help us move with integrity.
Place us on level ground, O Redeemer.
Move us to sing songs of thanksgiving
and to proclaim your wondrous deeds.

OPENING PRAYER (*Hebrews 1, 2; Job 2*)
Gracious God, through whom all things exist,
we are mindful this day
of siblings in faith around the world.
We rejoice in our oneness with them.
We are mindful, too,
of those near at hand and those far away—
those who suffer from ills and calamities,
from wars and disasters.
Be present with them and us, we pray—
even as you fix our hearts on you
and how we might, in faith,
respond to the needs of neighbors
around the world. Amen.

PROCLAMATION AND RESPONSE

PRAYER OF CONFESSION (Psalm 26; Hebrews 1, 2)
We are conscious this day, O God,
of the world's great needs:
for love,
for caring,
for right relationships of all kinds.
We are conscious, too, of the times we fall short:
the small daily choices
and the large systems in society
that impede the loving world you envision.
Save us from hypocrisy, we pray,
and help us find the places your glory abides.
Amen.

WORDS OF ASSURANCE (Hebrews 1, 2)
The psalmist says God made humanity
but a little lower than the angels.
We are, God knows, sometimes not even close
to angels at all.
Yet, God crowns us with glory and honor.
In the name of that Jesus, the perfecter of our salvation,
know that you are loved and forgiven. Amen.

PASSING THE PEACE OF CHRIST (Hebrews 1, 2)
On this World Communion Sunday, we honor the One
who created worlds and sustains all things through
the divine Word. As we share signs of peace with one
another, imagine the deep, creative love that extends—
through us, and by the power of the Holy Spirit—to siblings in every time and place.
The peace of Christ be with you.
And also with you.

RESPONSE TO THE WORD (Psalm 26)
Redeem us, O God,
Be gracious unto us and to the world.
In the great congregation,
    we will bless your holy name. Amen.

THANKSGIVING AND COMMUNION

INVITATION TO THE OFFERING (Psalm 26)
The psalmist invites us to walk in faithfulness before God. As part of this journey of faithfulness, with thanks for God's wondrous deeds, and in support of the church's ministry in this neighborhood and around the world, let us share our tithes and offerings.

OFFERING PRAYER (Hebrews 1, 2)
Holy God, creator of this and many other worlds,
    bless these gifts in Jesus' name,
        that they may aid a world of need, near and far.
Amen.

INVITATION TO COMMUNION (Hebrews 1, 2)
Scripture reminds us that Jesus, whom we remember in this meal, was and is the eternal Word, through whom God created the worlds. On this World Communion Sunday, Christians around the globe join us as we break the bread—at this same moment, and in time zones before and after us. Indeed, God's love stretches across time, space, and eternity. Let us gather at Christ's table.

SENDING FORTH

BENEDICTION (Job 2, Psalm 26)
Go forth, as God gives you strength,
    blameless and upright, persistent in integrity,
    trusting without wavering, and confident
    in God's love.
Go in peace. Amen.

October 13, 2024

Twenty-First Sunday after Pentecost
Proper 23

B. J. Beu
Copyright © B. J. Beu

COLOR

Green

SCRIPTURE READINGS

Job 23:1-9, 16-17; Psalm 22:1-15; Hebrews 4:12-16;
Mark 10:17-31

THEME IDEAS

There are times when we feel abandoned by God. While
Psalm 139 wonders where we can flee from God's presence, Job 23 and Psalm 22 wonder where God can be
found when calamity strikes. In Hebrews, Jesus sympathizes with us in our weakness. Indeed, during his
darkest hour, Jesus quotes Psalm 22 while hanging on
the cross. And in today's Gospel reading, a man blessed
with riches, a man who has obeyed the commandments
since his youth, wonders what he must do to be saved.
This is not a question you ask if you feel connected
to God! While there is a time for praise, these lections

remind us that there is also a time for grief, a time for calling out our woes to the One who often seems far away.

INVITATION AND GATHERING

CENTERING WORDS (Psalm 2)

Where do you go, Elusive One, when all hope fades?
Be with us in our time of need
and do not take your Holy Spirit from us.

CALL TO WORSHIP (Job 23, Psalm 22, Hebrews 4)

Where do we turn when our cries go unanswered?
**Where do we turn
when we feel forsaken and alone?**
We search for God before and behind us,
but God is not there.
**We search for God above and beneath us,
but come away empty.**
Yet even now, we will commit ourselves to God.
Even now, we will put our trust in the Lord.
Come! Let us worship.

OPENING PRAYER (Job 23, Psalm 22, Hebrews 4)

Elusive One, be near us in our need.
For we are poured out like water
and our hearts melt like wax within us.
You have watched over us since our birth
as a mother watches over her children.
Come to us swiftly and be with us now,
for the darkness threatens and the light fades.
Help us in our weakness
and touch us with your mercy and your grace.
Amen.

PROCLAMATION AND RESPONSE

PRAYER OF YEARNING (Mark 10)
You set before us the ways of life and death, O God.
Help us keep to your path
    when the road is hard and the cost seems high.
We yearn to touch your perfect love,
    if only it didn't mean giving up our comfort
      and our privilege.
We long to love you with perfect devotion,
    but we are loathe to alter our selfish ways.
Lift us beyond the empty shells of our shut-up hearts
    and help us find our way home.
For in your love, all things are possible. Amen.

WORDS OF ASSURANCE (Mark 10)
Who can be saved?
With mortals, it is impossible.
But for God, all things are possible.
Thanks be to God!

PASSING THE PEACE OF CHRIST (Hebrews 4)
Christ sympathizes with us in our weakness and comes
to us in our need. In gratitude for this great gift, let us
share signs of Christ's peace with one another.

INTRODUCTION TO THE WORD (Hebrews 4:12-13 CEB)
The author to the Hebrews writes: "God's word is living,
active, and sharper than any two-edged sword. It pene-
trates to the point that it separates the soul from the spirit
and the joints from the marrow. It's able to judge the
heart's thoughts and intentions. No creature is hidden
from it, but rather everything is naked and exposed to
the eyes of the one to whom we have to give an answer."
Listen attentively for the word of God, and you will live.

RESPONSE TO THE WORD (Psalm 22)

Our ancestors trusted God and were delivered.
They cried out to the Lord and were saved.
By living their faith with hope,
    they were not put to shame.
May we do likewise, that we too may have life
    and have it abundantly.

THANKSGIVING AND COMMUNION

OFFERING PRAYER (Psalm 22, Mark 10)

Even when you seem far away, O God,
    you give us our daily bread
        and deliver us from evil.
May the gifts we bring before you this day
    be signs of our gratitude for your gifts.
Bless this offering,
    that our gifts may be vessels
        of your overflowing grace.
Through these gifts, may others come to know
    the joy of your salvation,
        through Christ, our Lord. Amen.

SENDING FORTH

BENEDICTION (Psalm 22, Hebrews 4)

Whenever we feel poured out like water,
    Christ offers us grace and mercy.
Whenever we feel abandoned and alone,
    Christ gives us hope and encouragement.
Christ is there when our need is great.
    Thanks be to God.

October 20, 2024

Twenty-Second Sunday after Pentecost
Proper 24

Mary Scifres
Copyright © Mary Scifres

COLOR

Green

SCRIPTURE READINGS

Job 38:1-7, (34-41); Psalm 104:1-9, 24, 35c;
Hebrews 5:1-10; Mark 10:35-45

THEME IDEAS

Even on this Ordinary Sunday when the scriptures sup-
posedly aren't interrelated, the juxtaposition of Christ's
divinity and humanity points to a wisdom expressed in
all four scriptures. Hebrews proposes that Christ is both
the highest high priest of all and also the most obedient
child of God. This echoes role modeling that God seems
to be asking of Job and Jesus seems to be asking of his disciples. The path to greatness is paved with humility, obe-
dience, and even servanthood. This path, oddly enough,
allows us to approach the greatness of God's throne and
God's creation with deeper reverence and understanding.

INVITATION AND GATHERING

CENTERING WORDS (*Job 38, Psalm 104, Mark 10*)
The fullness of God's glory is manifest in the stars above and the earth below. Even though our lives are small and fleeting in the vastness of the universe, God's glory shines in and through us.

CALL TO WORSHIP (*Psalm 104, Hebrews 5, Mark 10*)
Come into God's presence.
All are welcome here.
Come into God's glory.
God's glory is all around.
As Christ came before us,
we come to worship and to pray.
As Christ turned to God,
we bring our anguish and our tears.
As Christ came to serve,
we bring our humble hearts.
Come into God's presence.
All are welcome here.

OPENING PRAYER (*Job 38, Psalm 104, Mark 10*)
Sing into our hearts, Creator God,
as you sang your glory into creation.
Speak to our minds with wisdom of old.
Draw us into your presence,
that we may remember who we are
and whose we are. Amen.

PROCLAMATION AND RESPONSE

PRAYER OF YEARNING (Job 38, Psalm 104, Hebrews 5, Mark 10)
Great and mighty God, create us anew this day.
When we pose as greater and mightier than we are,
    help us be humble and of service in your name.
When pride causes us to stumble,
    strengthen our faith.
When fear and shame cause us to shrink,
    remind us that we are made in your image.
Reclaim us as the people you have created us to be,
    and lead us back to the path of discipleship
        you have called us to walk.
In your great and gracious love, we pray. Amen.

WORDS OF ASSURANCE (Hebrews 5)
Christ's love and mercy are greater than our sins,
reconciling us to God and to one another.

PASSING THE PEACE OF CHRIST (Mark 10)
As Christ came to serve, so now Christ invites us to
serve one another with peace and love. Share signs of
this service with words of peace and acts of love.

INTRODUCTION TO THE WORD (Job 38)
Although we weren't around when the earth's founda-
tions were laid, God invites us into acts of creation each
and every day. Although our thoughts aren't as mighty
as God's, God invites us to learn from God's holy word.
Let's open our hearts and minds to the wisdom God is
sharing this day.

RESPONSE TO THE WORD (Psalm 104, Mark 10)
Bless God with every fiber of your being.
We will honor God with every breath we take.
Serve God by serving and loving God's world.
We will serve God's people each day.

THANKSGIVING AND COMMUNION

INVITATION TO THE OFFERING (Hebrews 5, Mark 10)
In service and love, may we bring our hearts, our offerings, and our gifts to God and to God's church.

OFFERING PRAYER (Job 38, Psalm 104)
Great and gracious God,
as you have blessed our lives and all of creation,
bless the gifts we now return to you.
Bless our hands and our lives,
that they may serve you and your creation.
Continue creating life and hope
through our offerings and our ministries.
May your glory and your grace
shine through everything we give,
everything we say,
and everything we do.
In loving gratitude, we pray. Amen.

SENDING FORTH

BENEDICTION (Psalm 104, Mark 10)
Go now to serve.
We go now to love.
Go with the blessing of God.
We go to be blessings to the world.

October 27, 2024

Twenty-Third Sunday after Pentecost
Reformation Sunday
Proper 25

Michael Beu
Copyright © Michael Beu

COLOR

Green

SCRIPTURE READINGS

Job 42:1-6, 10-17; Psalm 34:1-8, (19-22); Hebrews 7:23-28;
Mark 10:46-52

THEME IDEAS

Job 42 and Psalm 34 present an honest picture of the life
of faith. While the psalmist insists that God spares and
protects the righteous, Job is a chilling example of the
devastation that can befall even those whose righteousness is beyond reproach. The text suggests that Job's
ultimate vindication and the restoration of his fortunes
more than compensate him for what he lost when God
tested his faithfulness. But such assurances ring hollow.
If these texts are used, they must not be sugar coated,
lest we trivialize the suffering of the innocent. In today's

Gospel, blind Bartimaeus is offered anything he asks for. Not surprisingly he asks for the return of his physical sight. If we were Job or Bartimaeus, what would we ask for: our children back, our sight returned? Or would we ask to see with God's eyes or to truly taste the sweetness of God's salvation? What do we seek and how well do we really see?

INVITATION AND GATHERING

CENTERING WORDS (Psalm 34)

Taste and see that the Lord is good. God's steadfast love endures forever.

CALL TO WORSHIP (Job 42, Psalm 34)

Magnify the Lord.
> **Praise God's holy name.**

The Lord hears the pleas of the perishing.
> **God transforms our suffering into songs of joy.**

God restores our fortunes when calamity strikes.
> **Bless the Lord and praise God's holy name!**

OPENING PRAYER (Job 42, Mark 10)

Source of healing and mercy,
> heed us when we cry out in our need.

Give us the wisdom and the courage
> to accept the limits of our understanding,
>> as Job did before us.

Give us the confidence to sing your praises,
> even when fear and doubt darken our thoughts.

Grant us your healing balm, O God,
> that we may be made well
>> and follow you all the days of our lives. Amen.

PROCLAMATION AND RESPONSE

PRAYER OF YEARNING (Job 42, Psalm 34, Mark 10)
God of quiet mystery, we come looking for a blessing.
We long to be counted among the wise,
 but often find ourselves among the foolish,
  speaking without knowledge.
We yearn to be found among the righteous,
 but often travel with those who boast without cause.
We desire to be instruments of your grace,
 but often meet genuine pain with empty words.
As blind Bartimaeus before us,
 grant us the courage to cry out in our need,
  for you are ever drawing near to make us whole.
Amen.

WORDS OF ASSURANCE (Hebrews 7)
Draw near to God in Christ,
 and God will draw near to you.

PASSING THE PEACE OF CHRIST (Psalm 34)
Even in our darkest hours when God seems far away,
the grace and mercy of Christ are in our midst when we
share greetings of peace in his name. Let us share these
gifts with one another by passing the peace of Christ.

RESPONSE TO THE WORD (Mark 10)
Heed not the crowd nor those who would silence you.
 We will shout out our needs
 and the deepest desires of our hearts,
 for Christ is here to save us.
Make Christ the center of your lives.
 We will live in his grace and be whole.

THANKSGIVING AND COMMUNION

OFFERING PRAYER (*Job 42, Psalm 34, Mark 10*)
>Mighty God, as you restore sight to the blind
>>and healing to the afflicted,
>>>use these offerings to provide refuge for the lost
>>>and mercy for those who suffer.
>May our gifts find those who cry out in need
>>and who seek you with receptive hearts. Amen.

SENDING FORTH

BENEDICTION (*Psalm 34, Hebrews 7*)
>God heals the broken and makes the wounded whole.
>>**We go with peace in our hearts.**
>God finds the lost and gives them a home.
>>**We go with joy and thanksgiving.**
>God visits the lonely and makes them family.
>>**We go with as the people of God.**

November 3, 2024

Twenty-Fourth Sunday after Pentecost
All Saints Sunday/Proper 26

B. J. Beu
Copyright © B. J. Beu

COLOR

White

SCRIPTURE READINGS

Isaiah 25:6-9; Psalm 24; Revelation 21:1-6a; John 11:32-44

ALTERNATE SCRIPTURE READINGS FOR THE 23rd SUNDAY AFTER PENTECOST

Ruth 1:1-18; Psalm 146:1-10; Hebrews 9:11-14;
Mark 12:28-34
See The Abingdon Worship Annual 2021 *for ideas related to these readings.*

THEME IDEAS

All Saints Day celebrates those who have died in the faith. Today's scriptures reference the end time when there will be a new heaven and a new earth—a time when God will wipe away every tear. It is a time to celebrate the heavenly banquet, a banquet with rich food and aged wine. It is a time when weeping and mourning will be no more. The story of Jesus raising Lazarus from the dead is a sign of God's power over death itself. We have nothing to fear from the grave.

INVITATION AND GATHERING

CENTERING WORDS *(Revelation 21, John 11)*
Rejoice, saints of God. Death is swallowed up in everlasting life.

CALL TO WORSHIP *(Isaiah 25, Psalm 24, Revelation 21)*
Lift up your heads, O gates.
The King of glory has come.
Mourning and death shall be no more.
Feast on rich food and fine wine.
Come! Let us worship the God of our salvation.

OPENING PRAYER *(Isaiah 25, Psalm 24, Revelation 21)*
God of new beginnings, wipe away our tears,
    that we may come before your throne
        with hearts full of song
            and with souls on fire.
Help us live as those who are prepared to die,
    so when our time to depart comes
        we may go forth
            as those who are prepared to live.
Whether living or dying, O Lord,
    our hearts will always belong to you. Amen.

PROCLAMATION AND RESPONSE

PRAYER OF YEARNING (Isaiah 25:9b, Revelation 21, John 11)

> You know our grief, wellspring of tears,
> and our longing to see your face.
> We long for you to come down and save us.
> In our sorrow and pain,
> we yearn to be touched by healing love.
> As Lazarus before us,
> we need your hand to lift us from tombs
> that keep us from truly living.
> Open our mouths to exclaim with delight:
> "Here is our God for whom we have waited!"
> Amen.

WORDS OF ASSURANCE (Isaiah 25, Revelation 21)

> The vision of a new heaven and a new earth is sure.
> The one who prepares a banquet before us,
> a feast of rich food and fine wine,
> will wipe away our tears.
> Rejoice and be glad.
> The King of glory is the author of our salvation.

PASSING THE PEACE OF CHRIST (Isaiah 25, Revelation 21)

> God wipes away our tears, bestowing blessings upon us. Let us share signs of these blessings as we rejoice in the peace and fellowship of the saints of God.

INTRODUCTION TO THE WORD (Revelation 21)

> The word of God is trustworthy and true. Listen for the word of God.

RESPONSE TO THE WORD (Isaiah 25, John 11)
> Those who believe will see the glory of God.
> Let us recommit ourselves to this truth
>> as we celebrate the saints of God
>> and renew our faith in the One they served.

THANKSGIVING AND COMMUNION

OFFERING PRAYER (Isaiah 25, Revelation 21)
> God of abundance, you bless us with rich food
>> and fine wines at your banquet table.
> May our offering nourish the bodies and souls
>> of those who know only hunger and want.
> Bless our gifts into your holy service,
>> that all may come to know
>>> the blessings of your table
>>>> and the wonder of your love. Amen.

SENDING FORTH

BENEDICTION (Psalm 24, Revelation 21)
> Hold fast to the faith of God's saints, past and present.
>> **In our living and in our dying,**
>> **we belong to God.**
> Trust the example they left for us to follow.
>> **In our loving and in our service,**
>> **we are heirs with Christ.**
> Walk in the puddles of light
> the saints left as footprints for us to follow.
>> **In our journeys of faith,**
>> **we are one in the Spirit,**
>> **we are one in the Lord.**

November 10, 2024

Twenty-Fifth Sunday after Pentecost
Proper 27

B. J. Beu
Copyright © B. J. Beu

COLOR

Green

SCRIPTURE READINGS

Ruth 3:1-5; 4:13-17; Psalm 127; Hebrews 9:24-28;
Mark 12:38-44

THEME IDEAS

"Unless it is the Lord who builds the house, the builders' work is pointless" (Psalm 127:1 CEB). Naomi thinks she is building a house for herself and for Ruth, but God is building a house for the whole people of Israel. The psalmist reminds us that children are a heritage from God—but a heritage, as Naomi found out, that can disappear at any moment. Hebrews reminds us that our hopes are founded on Christ, not on any sanctuary built with human hands. Finally, while the Temple system relies upon human generosity, God views the humble offering of a poor widow to be of infinitely greater value than the largess of the rich. As the Pharisees show, human

219

scheming and posturing only go so far. Unless God builds the house, the builders labor in vain.

INVITATION AND GATHERING

CENTERING WORDS (Psalm 127:1 CEB)

"Unless it is the Lord who builds the house, the builders' work is pointless."

CALL TO WORSHIP (Psalm 127:1 NIV)

Unless the Lord builds the house,
the builders labor in vain.
Build us into a spiritual house, O God,
and we will be a holy people.
Unless the Lord guards the city,
the guards keep watch in vain.
Guard our hearts and minds,
that we may walk in your ways.
Unless the Lord is the center of our worship,
our words and praise are in vain.
Here and now, Holy One,
may we taste eternity.

OPENING PRAYER (Ruth 3–4, Psalm 127, Hebrews 9, Mark 12)

God of infinite possibilities, when the world says, "No,"
you say, "Yes!"
The world warns against marrying foreigners,
but you transform honest love
into a blessing for all people.
The world lauds the industry of the rich,
but you cherish the sacrifice of the poor.
Build us into a household of love
and guard the walls of our spirit,
that we may remain strong
in service to one another. Amen.

PROCLAMATION AND RESPONSE

PRAYER OF YEARNING (Mark 12)
Holy Seer, we long to perceive ourselves
  as you see us.
We yearn to look through your eyes
  and envision who you created us to be.
Help us love ourselves,
  that we may truly love others.
Help us give freely from our bounty,
  that we may rejoice in the gifts of others,
    even when they seem small by comparison.
In Christ's name, we pray. Amen.

WORDS OF ASSURANCE (Psalm 127, Mark 12)
Even the smallest gift is precious to God
  when we share what little we have to give.
Even the smallest gesture is holy in God's sight
  when it is offered with great love.
Rejoice, God is building us into a spiritual house,
  a house of infinite worth.

PASSING THE PEACE OF CHRIST (Psalm 127)
God is building our lives into a spiritual house of love,
hope, and blessing. Let us rejoice in God, our builder, as
we share signs of Christ's peace with one another.

RESPONSE TO THE WORD (Ruth 3–4)
Securing a husband for Ruth,
  Naomi secured the security of Israel
  through her descendent, King David.
Miracles abound when we follow our hearts
  and act with great love.
Be more than hearers of the word of God—
  live the Word each and every day.

When we live in the love of God,
we build the realm of God.

THANKSGIVING AND COMMUNION

OFFERING PRAYER (Ruth 3–4, Mark 12)

Free our hearts, gracious God,
that your great purposes may work through our love,
as they did for Naomi and Ruth before us.
Multiply our gifts, Holy One,
that all people may be built into a spiritual house—
a house that no one can bring down. Amen.

SENDING FORTH

BENEDICTION (Psalm 127, Hebrews 9)

May God build you into a spiritual house
to be a shelter for those in need.
Become a fortress housing God's Spirit.
Touch the hearts of those you meet
and heal the world.
Go with God's blessing.

November 17, 2024

Twenty-Sixth Sunday after Pentecost
Proper 28

Mary Scifres
Copyright © Mary Scifres

COLOR

Green

SCRIPTURE READINGS

1 Samuel 1:4-20; 1 Samuel 2:1-10; Hebrews 10:11-14, (15-18), 19-25; Mark 13:1-8

THEME IDEAS

God's faithfulness emerges in each of today's readings. The world may crumble and buildings may fall, but God's faithfulness and strength will uphold us in the midst of turmoil. A woman may be barren and distraught, but God's faithfulness, love, and healing will bring comfort. We may feel shame and regret for our shortcomings, but God's faithfulness, mercy, and grace will draw us closer to God. God's faithfulness is our foundation and will sustain us, no matter how fragile our lives or our world.

INVITATION AND GATHERING

CENTERING WORDS *(1 Samuel 2, Hebrews 10, Mark 13)*
How great is our God? Great enough to hold us when
we fall down. Great enough to love us when we feel un-
lovable. Great enough to sustain and strengthen us all
the days of our lives.

CALL TO WORSHIP *(1 Samuel 1, 1 Samuel 2, Hebrews 10,
Mark 13)*
We approach the God of grace and glory,
who has called us to worship this day.
We arrive from the chaos of our world
into the clarity of God's presence.
We leave the struggles of our lives
to embrace the power of God's love.
May this hour bring us courage
and a time to strengthen our faith.

OPENING PRAYER *(1 Samuel 2, Hebrews 10, Mark 13,
Hebrews 12:1)*
Great and mighty God, open our hearts
to the power of your Holy Spirit.
Open our minds to the wisdom of your Word.
Help us run the race of life with faithful perseverance
and with steadfast love. Amen.

PROCLAMATION AND RESPONSE

PRAYER OF YEARNING *(1 Samuel 1, 1 Samuel 2,
Hebrews 10, Mark 13)*
Gracious God, hear the anguish of our hearts.
Comfort us when our souls feel barren, shriveled,
and lifeless.

Strengthen us when we feel lost and alone.
Heal us when we hurt and misuse ourselves
    and others.
Guide us into your strong arms of love,
    that we may receive your gracious mercy
        and rest in your powerful love.
In hope and gratitude, we pray. Amen.

WORDS OF ASSURANCE (Hebrews 10)

Hold onto hope, for God is faithful and true.
The promise of love is ours,
    through the grace of Christ Jesus
    and the power of the Holy Spirit.
Thanks be to God!

PASSING THE PEACE OF CHRIST (Hebrews 10)

As you share signs of peace, spark acts of love and good
deeds everywhere you go.

RESPONSE TO THE WORD (1 Samuel 2)

May our hearts rejoice in God.
    May our faith embrace God's power.
Hold onto hope.
    God's promises are faithful and true.

PRAYER OF RESPONSE (1 Samuel 2)

God of power and might, lift up the lowly of our world.
Raise the poor from the dust
    and offer provision for the least and the last.
But don't let us off the hook.
Work in and through us.
For we too can lift up the poor
    and meet the needs of the least and the last.
Guard our lives and strengthen our faith,
    that we may be strong in love and justice
        for all your creation.
In hope and trust, we pray. Amen.

THANKSGIVING AND COMMUNION

INVITATION TO THE OFFERING (1 Samuel 1)
God doesn't ask us to give our first-born child or the last cent we own. God asks for hearts of generosity and gifts lovingly given. Out of gratitude for God's trustworthy love and generous gifts, let us return gifts of gratitude to God.

OFFERING PRAYER (1 Samuel 1, 1 Samuel 2, Hebrews 10)
Faithful and loving God,
    thank you for blessing us and our world
        in so many amazing ways.
Bless the gifts we return to you now,
    that they may be blessings of hope
        and signs of your faithfulness
            for all the world to know. Amen.

SENDING FORTH

BENEDICTION (1 Samuel 2, Hebrews 10, Mark 13)
Go into the world with hope.
    We will shine with God's glory and grace.
Courageously face the struggles and joys of each day.
    We will embrace the power of God's love.
Go forth in courage and faith.
    We will bring God's love to the world.

November 24, 2024

Christ the King/Reign of Christ Sunday
Proper 29

B. J. Beu
Copyright © B. J. Beu

COLOR

White

SCRIPTURE READINGS

2 Samuel 23:1-7; Psalm 132:1-12, (13-18);
Revelation 1:4b-8; John 18:33-37

THEME IDEAS

Kingship, both human and divine, focuses today's readings. Though a flawed vessel, King David is portrayed as
an ideal king and ruler. Second Samuel concludes with a
recitation of God's everlasting covenant to David's house
and lineage. In Psalm 132, David forswears sleep until a
resting place is found for the ark of God. Yet, even David's piety, and God's promise of an everlasting covenant,
cannot keep David's line from falling into self-destruc-
tion. Divine kingship alone is faithful. Revelation 1 and
John 18 herald this kingship. Ultimately, all human rulers
fail us. Christ alone is our rightful King and sovereign.

INVITATION AND GATHERING

CENTERING WORDS (Revelation 1, John 18)
> All human leaders will one day disappoint and fail us.
> Divine kingship alone is faithful.

CALL TO WORSHIP (Revelation 1, John 18)
> When leaders disappoint and fail us,
> > **turn to Christ, who is always faithful.**
> When deceitful words appeal to our baser instincts,
> > **hearken to Christ and the clarion call**
> > **of our better angels.**
> When charlatans seek our allegiance,
> > **hold fast to Christ, our rightful Lord and King.**

–OR–

CALL TO WORSHIP (2 Samuel 23, Psalm 132, John 18)
> Christ comes to be our King.
> > **We are here to be Christ's people.**
> Clothed in righteousness, Christ comes to save us.
> > **Let the faithful shout for joy.**
> Adorned with the glory of the rising sun,
> > **Christ disperses our gloom with holy light.**
> Let all God's people proclaim the Prince of Peace.

OPENING PRAYER (2 Samuel 23, Revelation 1)
> Sovereign God, you clothe your people
> > in the garments of salvation,
> > > and you bless them with grace and peace.
> Open our eyes to the glory of your Son,
> > who comes to rule with justice
> > > and reign with righteousness.
> Open our ears to the sound of his voice,
> > and open our hearts to love as he loves,
> > > that we might shine like dew on the grass.
> > > and dwell in Christ's peace. Amen.

PROCLAMATION AND RESPONSE

PRAYER OF YEARNING (Mark 12)
Mighty God, you are the bedrock of our lives
　　and the source of our wisdom and strength.
When we lose our way,
　　help us follow your guidance
　　　　and embrace your rule in our lives.
When we build our lives on shifting sand,
　　fix our gaze on Christ's kingdom,
　　　　that we might build our future
　　　　　　on the solid foundation of Christ,
　　　　　　　　our rock and our cornerstone. Amen.

WORDS OF ASSURANCE (Psalm 132, Mark 12)
God's promise of faithful love to King David
　　and his descendants is fulfilled through Christ.
Christ' kingship is faithful,
　　abounding in steadfast love.

PASSING THE PEACE OF CHRIST (Revelation 1)
Christ's glory fills the skies and gladdens the heart. Let
us offer signs of kinship in Christ's name by exchanging
the peace of Christ.

RESPONSE TO THE WORD (2 Samuel 23)
The Spirit of the Lord speaks to us,
teaching us lessons that endure.
　　The King of kings calls to us,
　　beckoning us to follow.
The Light of light shines on us,
making wise the simple.
　　The Spirit of the Lord speaks to us,
　　leading us into life.
May we embrace the word of God this day,
and may we live it every moment of our lives.

THANKSGIVING AND COMMUNION

INVITATION TO THE OFFERING (Revelation 1)
>The Alpha and Omega, the first and the last, the one who was and is and is to come, invites us to share our blessings with others, as we collect our tithes and offerings.

OFFERING PRAYER (2 Samuel 23, Psalm 132)
>Strong One of Israel, you bless our lives with splendor:
>>sunlight sparkling on the water,
>>dew on the grass,
>>trees etched against the night sky.
>
>May our gifts and offerings reflect our gratitude
>>for the wonder you bring to our lives.
>
>And may those who receive these gifts
>>come to know your bounty
>>and the glory of your kingdom. Amen.

SENDING FORTH

BENEDICTION (2 Samuel 23, Psalm 132, Revelation 1, John 18)
>The Mighty One of Israel is faithful.
>>**God's promises are sure.**
>
>The rock of our salvation is strong and true.
>>**Christ's kingdom never ends.**
>
>The Spirit guides and guards us.
>>**The Spirit's love leads us home.**

November 28, 2024

Thanksgiving Day

Silvia Purdie

COLOR

Red

SCRIPTURE READINGS

Joel 2:21-27; Psalm 126; 1 Timothy 2:1-7; Matthew 6:25-33

THEME IDEA

Rejoice and give thanks! This is a day to remember the gifts and blessings that God showers in our lives. This is a season to trust God's providential care and to rest assured that we are held in Christ's gentle arms of love. In a world that instills fear and worry that nothing we have will ever be enough, we discover in Christ's arms that we have everything we need.
(Mary Scifres)

INVITATION AND GATHERING

CENTERING WORDS (Joel 2:27a, CEB)
"You will know that I am in the midst of Israel, and that I am the Lord your God—no other exists" (Joel 2:27).

CALL TO WORSHIP *(Psalm 126:3)*
When the Lord turned the tide of history,
we could hardly believe it!
Laughter bubbled within us;
shouts of joy burst forth:
"The Lord has done great things for us."
Let us worship the Lord.

PROCLAMATION AND RESPONSE

PRAYER OF CONFESSION *(Matthew 6)*
O God, we long to come into your presence
undistracted by our hectic lives.
But instead, we fight our way in,
amidst the clutter and stress.
Our minds are full of worry.
Our hearts are buffeted this way and that.
Our souls are tired and sore.
We yearn to rest in the assurance of Jesus:
"Look at the birds of the air.
Your heavenly Father feeds them.
You are even more precious to God!
Consider the lilies of the field.
Even Solomon in all his glory was not dressed
so fine!"
O God, you know our need.
Grow our vision and nurture our trust
until our worries fall away.
Restore us in your grace that we may breathe again,
through Christ and in his righteousness. Amen.

RESPONSE TO THE WORD
Remember this day the gifts and blessings
that God showers in our lives.

This is a season to trust God's providential care
    and to rest assured in Christ's arms of love.
In those arms, we have everything we need.
Rejoice and give thanks!
(Mary Scifres)

THANKSGIVING AND COMMUNION

OFFERING PRAYER

Gracious and abundant God, like the birds of the air,
    we can trust your provision.
You take care of us.
Like the lilies of the field,
    all that we have is yours.
Every good thing is a gift from you.
You take care of us.
Bless us this Thanksgiving day,
    and bless the gifts we bring,
        that in all we make and say and do:
            trust may grow, beauty may flourish,
            generosity may flow,
                and your name may be praised.
Through Jesus Christ our Lord, we pray. Amen.

COMMUNION LITURGY(1 Timothy 2)

We proclaim with those in every age and tongue:
    There is one God.
And we affirm our faith in the one mediator
between God and humanity,
    Jesus Christ, God made human.
Jesus gave himself and all he was
on our behalf.
    Halleluia! Thanks be to God!
Thanks be to the Lord Jesus, our friend,
    who came to us, to be one of us,
    to show us the way, and to reveal all truth.

Thank you, Jesus, that your heart and your desire
    is for everyone to be saved, rescued, released,
    and come to the truth.
You showed this truth in your touch, your words,
    and your actions.
You revealed this truth in the breaking of bread.
Thank you, Jesus, that you gathered
    with your friends on the night before you died.
You shared with them your love and your pain,
    and you took the bread and broke it, saying:
    "Eat this bread which is broken for you.
    It will be for you my body, the bread of life."
Thank you Jesus that you gather us
    in your continual prayer of thanks
    and in your communion with the Father.
We come freely and with open hearts,
    in communion with the Father, and the Son,
    and the Holy Spirit,
    because you gave your all for us. Amen.
Friends, we share in the life of God
    through these holy gifts—
    gifts that are right and acceptable
    in the sight of God.

SENDING FORTH

BENEDICTION
Friends, do not worry about food or drink or clothes.
Do not fret about your health or your bank account,
    about jobs to do or things to plan.
Do not worry about the state of the world,
    about the changing climate
    or the very real threats we face.
Choose instead to focus on God.

Hold your gaze on Christ.
Tune your ear to his words.
Throw your energy into his ways
    and you will be held.
You will be okay, no matter what comes.
For you are loved more than you can know.
Go in peace.

–OR–

BENEDICTION

This Thanksgiving, be filled with thanks and praise.
Let it overflow, bursting through every stress
    and anxiety.
May it trickle gently over every grief and sadness,
    until thanks and praise are in every word you say,
    every choice you make, every moment you live.
Glory and praise to God.
Peace be with you.

December 1, 2024

First Sunday of Advent

Mary Petrina Boyd

COLOR

Purple

SCRIPTURE READINGS

Jeremiah 33:14-16; Psalm 25:1-10;
1 Thessalonians 3:9-13; Luke 21:25-36

THEME IDEAS

These passages speak of God's faithful promise of justice and righteousness. To people who had lost all hope, Jeremiah promises that God will keep them safe. Knowing God's promises, the psalmist expresses profound trust in God. Paul rejoices in the community of love. Jesus reminds folk of the promise that God's kingdom is near.

INVITATION AND GATHERING

CENTERING WORDS (Luke 21)

The kingdom of God is close at hand. Be alert and see the signs of hope.

CALL TO WORSHIP (Jeremiah 33, Luke 21)
> As we journey through the Sundays of Advent,
> listen to the promises of God:
>> **a righteous branch springs forth,**
> a promise of justice and righteousness,
>> **a promise of safety.**
> Listen to the promise of Jesus:
>> **the kingdom of God draws near.**
> Keep alert; watch for signs of hope.
>> **Our Advent journey begins.**

–OR–

CALL TO WORSHIP (Jeremiah 33, Luke 21)
> Wait for God.
>> **We wait for the promise of new life.**
> Wait for God.
>> **We wait for the promise of security.**
> Wait for God.
>> **We wait for God's love to be born anew.**
> God's love is everlasting.
>> **God's promises are true.**

–OR–

CALL TO WORSHIP (Jeremiah 33)
> The days are coming, God promises.
>> **New life will spring forth.**
> The days are coming, God affirms.
>> **We will live in safety.**
> The days are coming, God assures.
>> **Justice and righteousness will reign everywhere.**
> God's promises are true.
>> **Let us rejoice!**

OPENING PRAYER (*Luke 21*)

God of every season,
>   as we begin our journey through Advent,
>>   turn our hearts toward you.

Guide us into your realm of peace and joy.
Teach us to set aside our worries,
>   as we walk in faithfulness and trust.

May the love within us be born anew.
Help us remain alert,
>   that we may respond to pain and suffering
>>   and notice the signs of abundant life
>>>   all around us.

Come, Lord Jesus; come to us now, we pray. Amen.

PROCLAMATION AND RESPONSE

PRAYER OF YEARNING (*Psalm 25, Luke 21*)

Compassionate God, show us your ways.
Guide us in your paths
>   and lead us in your truth.

For your love is faithful,
>   and your will brings us abundant life.

It is easy to be distracted
>   during this busy time of year.

The worries of life threaten to overwhelm us.
Remind us of who we are meant to be:
>   merciful, faithful, patient, and loving.

We will place our trust in you,
>   no matter what happens.

May we forget our past mistakes
>   and live into a future filled with love. Amen.

WORDS OF ASSURANCE (*Psalm 25*)

God's mercy and steadfast love are eternal.
God shows us the way to abundant life.

PASSING THE PEACE OF CHRIST (1 Thessalonians 3)
May God increase our love for one another and strengthen our hearts in holiness, as we greet one another in peace.

PRAYER OF PREPARATION (Psalm 25)
O God, help us know your ways.
Teach us your paths
and lead us in your truth.
As we hear these scriptures,
may they open our hearts
to your life-giving grace. Amen.

RESPONSE TO THE WORD (Psalm 25, Luke 21)
Faithful God, your promises are true.
We trust you completely.
You guide our steps,
offering us forgiveness and new beginnings.
Ground our lives in your love
and keep us alert,
that we may see the signs
of your transforming presence. Amen.

THANKSGIVING AND COMMUNION

INVITATION TO THE OFFERING (Jeremiah 33)
As God promises to execute justice and righteousness in the world, God invites us to help make this promise a reality. Let us offer our gifts and our lives, that all may be blessed.

OFFERING PRAYER (1 Thessalonians 3)
We thank you, God, for the joy we feel this day.
We are blessed by this community of love,
this sanctuary of acceptance.

We place our trust in you,
>knowing that you care for us.
With deep gratitude for all you provide to us,
>we offer our gifts to you.
Centered our hearts during this season of giving.
Amen.

GREAT THANKSGIVING

May God lead you.
>**May God guide you.**
We rejoice this day!
>**We rejoice in God!**
Thank you, God.
>**Thank you for all you are and all you do.**

We thank you, loving God,
>for your presence in our lives and in our world.
At the beginning of time, you called forth your creation:
>planets, sun and stars, plants and animals,
>and all the wonderful, amazing variety
>of your creatures.
We know that you are at work in our world,
>repairing what is broken and inviting us to join you.
You show us the way that leads to life and hope.
Yet, we often turn away from you
>and follow the devices of our hearts.
We fail to love you as we should,
>just as we fail to love your people.
Yet, your love was always there, always steadfast.
You sent prophets to teach us your ways.
When we wandered away from you,
>they called us back.
When we were discouraged, they offered us hope.

And so, with your people, in all ages and all places,
we join the heavenly chorus, as we proclaim:
>   **Holy, holy, holy, God of power and strength.**
>   **Creation and heaven are filled with your glory.**
>   **Hosanna in the highest.**
>   **Blessed is Jesus, who comes in your name.**
>   **Hosanna in the highest.**

Out of love for us, you sent Jesus to walk with us.
He is your Word, your living presence in the world.
He taught us to love one another
>   and to extend this love to all creation.
He proclaimed that your kingdom was near—
>   a realm of justice and righteousness,
>   where all may find abundant life.
He taught us to see signs of your presence
>   in our lives.
He reminded us to be alert and ready.
The powerful were threatened
>   by his message of love and acceptance,
>   and they sought to destroy him.

And so, Jesus gathered for a last meal with his friends
>   and promised them his eternal presence.
He took bread, gave thanks to you, broke it,
>   and gave it saying:
>   "This is myself, my very being, given to you.
>   When you eat this, remember me."
When the supper was finished, Jesus took the cup,
>   gave thanks and offered it to his friends, saying:
>   "This is the cup of a new covenant of forgiveness.
>   It is poured out for you and for many.
When you drink this, remember me."

And so, grateful for Jesus, for his witness to love,
and for the precious gift of this shared meal,
we proclaim the mystery of faith:
Christ is. Christ was. Christ will be.

Pour out your blessing upon this bread, O God.
Wheat, grown in the fields, and touched by yeast,
becomes life-giving food.
This bread is transformed by your love
into the living presence of Jesus.
Pour out your blessing upon this cup,
juice from grapes grown in the sun.
May we drink deeply of the forgiveness Jesus offers.
Send your Spirit on this community,
gathered here around your table.
Feed us this very hour,
that we may truly become the body of Christ,
offering life to the world.
Through your beloved child, Jesus Christ,
and with the life-giving power of the Holy Spirit,
all honor and glory are yours,
now and forevermore.
Amen.

SENDING FORTH

BENEDICTION *(Luke 21)*
Be alert! God's realm of love and peace is breaking in.
Set aside all worries and let joy be yours.
God is with you.
Go in love.

December 8, 2024

Second Sunday of Advent

B. J. Beu
Copyright © B. J. Beu

COLOR

Purple

SCRIPTURE READINGS

Malachi 3:1-4; Luke 1:68-79; Philippians 1:3-11; Luke 3:1-6

THEME IDEAS

The message of God's salvation is like a refiner's fire or fullers' soap, cleansing us of our impurities. While the advent of the Messiah is marked with hopeful expectation, preparing for this arrival places demands on our lives. With words that confront our complacency, John the Baptist warns us to repent and amend our ways. Christ is coming, bringing hope, eagerness, and anticipation. But Christ's coming is also like a refiner's fire and fuller's soap, which should give us pause and fill us with trepidation.

243

INVITATION AND GATHERING

CENTERING WORDS *(Malachi 3)*

God's salvation is like a refiner's fire, cleansing our impurities and making us clean and blameless before the Lord.

CALL TO WORSHIP *(Luke 1, Luke 3)*

A voice cries in the wilderness:
"Prepare the way of the Lord!"
A challenge is uttered from on high:
"Make straight the paths of our God."
Every valley will be lifted up.
Every mountain will be made low.
The winding path will be made straight,
and every rough way will be made smooth.
Come! Let us worship the God of our salvation.

–OR–

CALL TO WORSHIP *(Luke 3)*

How shall we prepare for the coming of the Lord?
With hearts filled with love and peace.
How shall we prepare for the coming of Christ?
With prayers filled with adoration and devotion.
How shall we prepare for the coming of our savior?
With songs filled with joy and hope.
How shall we prepare for the coming of God's Son?
With worship filled with passion and spirit.

OPENING PRAYER *(Luke 1, Philippians 1, Luke 3)*

God of our deliverance, you meet us in our need.
You fill the valleys of our insecurities with hope
and bring low the mountains of our pride
and conceit.
As we await your Son and the glory of your salvation,
guide our feet in the ways of peace. Amen.

PROCLAMATION AND RESPONSE

PRAYER OF YEARNING (Malachi 3, Luke 1, Luke 3)
We need the tender mercy of your grace, Holy One,
    as we seek to comprehend the light of your love.
Disperse the shadows in our lives
    and release those who sit in darkness,
        that they may find peace and hope
           in the places where fear holds sway.
Come to us like a refiner's fire and fullers' soap,
    for we long to be purified in body and soul
        and made ready to see the light
           of your salvation. Amen.

WORDS OF ASSURANCE (Luke 1)
Christ brings light to our darkness
    and hope to disperse the shadow of death around us.
Seek the Lord and find life anew.

PASSING THE PEACE OF CHRIST (Philippians 1)
The one who brings the peace that passes all understanding awaits. Share the longing for this peace as you
share signs of Christ's love with one another.

INTRODUCTION TO THE WORD (Philippians 1)
The one who began a good work in us leads us into holiness and righteousness. Listen well, for God is speaking
still.

RESPONSE TO THE WORD or BENEDICTION
(Malachi 3, Luke 1, Luke 3)
Like a refiner's fire and fuller's soap,
    God cleanses our lives.
Like a glorious sunrise,
    God fills our darkness with light, love, and joy.

Like a merciful loving parent,
**God offers us second chances
and shows us the way home.**

THANKSGIVING AND COMMUNION

INVITATION TO THE OFFERING (Malachi, Luke 3)
As we prepare the way of the Lord, let us open our
hearts to share gifts of love and mercy—gifts that are
pleasing to our God.

OFFERING PRAYER (Malachi 3, Luke 1)
As you rescued your people of old,
rescue us over and over again, Mighty One.
As you purified the saints like a refiner's fire,
purify our lives this day and bless the gifts
we bring before you now.
Through our offering, may those who sit in darkness
find their way into the light
of your loving arms. Amen.

SENDING FORTH

BENEDICTION (Philippians 1)
May your love overflow in mercy and compassion,
as you walk in the ways of Christ.
May you produce a harvest of righteousness,
as you live as Christ's disciples to the glory of God.

December 15, 2024

Third Sunday of Advent

Karin Ellis

COLOR

Purple

SCRIPTURE READINGS

Zephaniah 3:14-20; Isaiah 12:2-6; Philippians 4:4-7;
Luke 3:7-18

THEME IDEAS

On this third Sunday of Advent, joy is prevalent
throughout our scriptures, but the Gospel also contains
a word of warning. The prophet Zephaniah reminds the
people to rejoice because God provides and God will
bring them home. Isaiah proclaims trust in God, which
is a great reason to sing God's praises. The letter to the
Philippians reminds us that when we trust God, when
we bring our whole selves to God, we dwell in God's
peace and rejoice in God's favor. The story from Luke
brings us the word of warning: be generous with those
in need and be fair in our dealings with others. There is
one coming who is greater than John and who has the
power to draw us into the ways of God.

INVITATION AND GATHERING

CENTERING WORDS *(Zephaniah 3, Isaiah 12)*
Rejoice and be glad! God is at work while we wait and hope and pray for God's peace to come upon the earth.

CALL TO WORSHIP *(Isaiah 12)*
Rejoice, for God is here!
God is our strength and our light.
Let us give thanks to God.
We will sing praises for all the earth to hear!

OPENING PRAYER *(Philippians 4)*
God of love and joy, thank you for your presence
in our lives.
During this time of worship,
draw us closer to you and to one another.
May we grow in our love for you and for our neighbor.
May we lay aside our worries,
trusting that you hear what lies in our hearts.
May we dwell in your peace
and be guided by the one who is to come,
your Son, Jesus Christ.
In your holy name, we pray. Amen.

PROCLAMATION AND RESPONSE

PRAYER OF YEARNING *(Luke 3)*
Merciful God, it can be hard to follow your ways.
We want to hold on to what we have.
We want to mind our own business
and ignore the needs of others.
We want to follow the ways of the world
and not your ways.

Remind us that you offer us forgiveness
and bring healing and redemption into our lives.
Help us turn to you once again,
that we may receive the good news
of your endless love and grace. Amen.

WORDS OF ASSURANCE (Philippians 4)

God hears our prayers and offers us forgiveness.
In the name of Christ, you are forgiven.
Thanks be to God! Amen.

PASSING THE PEACE OF CHRIST (Zephaniah 3, Luke 3)

God is in our midst and Christ brings peace and healing.
May the peace of Christ be with you.
And also with you!
In a spirit of joy, share the peace of Christ
with one another.

PRAYER OF PREPARATION (Philippians, Luke 3)

Holy One, open our ears to receive your word.
Open our hearts to receive your presence.
And open our hands to do your work in the world.
Amen.

RESPONSE TO THE WORD (Isaiah 12, Luke 3)

Prepare your hearts to receive Emmanuel in your lives.
**We will proclaim the good news of God
to all people.**
Let us rejoice and give thanks to God!
We will rejoice and sing God's praise forever!

THANKSGIVING

INVITATION TO THE OFFERING (Philippians 4)
God has given us so much. May we, in turn, bear good
fruit for God's world. In praise and thanksgiving, let us
open our hearts and offer our gifts to God.

OFFERING PRAYER (Luke 3)
Abundant God, we give you thanks for these gifts.
May you bless them and use them
    to feed the hungry, clothe the naked,
        and bring comfort to those in need.
And may we offer our very selves
    as we proclaim your good news
        of love and grace for all people. Amen.

SENDING FORTH

BENEDICTION (Zephaniah 3, Luke 3)
Brothers and sisters, siblings in Christ,
    God is truly with us.
Go forth, rejoicing that Christ shows us the way.
Go in peace.
Go in hope. Amen.

December 22, 2024

Fourth Sunday of Advent

Mary Scifres
Copyright © Mary Scifres

COLOR

Purple

SCRIPTURE READINGS

Micah 5:2-5a; Luke 1:46b-55; Hebrews 10:5-10;
Luke 1:39-45

THEME IDEAS

The pace of Advent quickens as Mary hastens to visit her elderly cousin, Elizabeth. Upon their meeting, Elizabeth's unborn child leaps with joy and the Holy Spirit fills Elizabeth's spirit with a joyous proclamation of faith. Mary responds with her own song of joyous faith, prompting us to embrace the celebration. We celebrate the arrival of the holy child—the one who reverses fortunes and re-creates the world with justice and peace.

INVITATION AND GATHERING

CENTERING WORDS (Luke 1)
> With fullness of heart, soul, and mind, we gather to glorify God and to rejoice in God, our Savior.

CALL TO WORSHIP (Luke 1, Micah 5)
> Rejoice in the presence and love of Christ.
> **We rejoice in the one who lives in our hearts.**
> Rejoice, for Christ brings justice and peace to our world.
> **We rejoice in the one who calls us to justice and peace.**
> Rejoice with faith and hope.
> **We rejoice in the one whose promises are true.**

CALL TO WORSHIP or RESPONSE TO THE WORD
(Luke 1, Micah 5)
> Christ's love has called us here.
> **Our spirits rejoice in God, our Savior.**
> Christ's love is transforming the world.
> **In joy, we'll give thanks and sing.**
> Christ's love calls us to justice and peace.
> **In faith, we'll answer the call.**

OPENING PRAYER (Luke 1, Micah 5)
> God of ancient days and future visions,
>> we come into your presence
>>> to celebrate the joy of your Holy Spirit
>>>> and the blessing of your Son, Christ Jesus.
> Fill us with your Holy Spirit,
>> as you filled Elizabeth long ago.
> Sing through our songs of joy,
>> as you sang through Mary.
> Speak through our words and our thoughts,
>> that we may grow closer to the justice and the peace
>>> of Christ Jesus, who calls us here today.
> In Christ's holy and blessed name, we pray. Amen.

PROCLAMATION AND RESPONSE

PRAYER OF YEARNING (Luke 1, Micah 5)

Merciful Savior, you know the hunger of our hearts,
 the hurt of our world,
  and the weakness of our lives.
Feed us with faith and hope.
Comfort us with love and joy.
Forgive us with your grace.
Strengthen us with your Spirit
 and give us the faith of Mary.
For we yearn to proclaim your promises
 and draw strength from your vision
  of justice and peace in our weary world.
In hope and trust, we pray. Amen.

WORDS OF ASSURANCE (Luke 1)

Christ's mercy is for you, my friends.
Christ's mercy is for me.
Christ's mercy and grace are sure and assuring.
May it be well with our souls. Amen.

PASSING THE PEACE OF CHRIST (Luke 1)

As Mary greeted Elizabeth , may we greet one another
with love. As Elizabeth greeted Mary, may we greet one
another with joy. In love and joy, share words of blessing
and signs of peace with one another.
*(Encourage online worshipers to share comments of peace and
joy on your video platform. If appropriate, invite all worshipers to take a moment to send a text message of joy and love to
someone who isn't in worship today.)*

RESPONSE TO THE WORD (Luke 1)

How do we magnify the Lord?
 With magnificent acts of love.

With quiet moments of grace.
With profound movements of justice.
With relationships of peace and forgiveness.
**With kindness to strangers
and food for the hungry.**
By lifting up the lowly and protecting the vulnerable.
By rejoicing in faith and trusting in love.
May our lives and our love reflect Christ's presence
and magnify the Lord.

THANKSGIVING AND COMMUNION

INVITATION TO THE OFFERING (Luke 1)
With joy and faith, may we bring our gifts and our love
before God in this time of offering.

OFFERING PRAYER (Luke 1, Micah 5)
May these gifts glorify your name, Holy One.
May the ministries we support
bring justice and peace to your world.
May they offer faith and hope to your people.
In grateful joy, we pray. Amen.

SENDING FORTH

BENEDICTION (Luke 1, Micah 5)
Go forth with joy.
Go forth in faith.
May peace be our way in the world.

December 24, 2024

Christmas Eve

Amy B. Hunter

COLOR

White

SCRIPTURE READINGS

Isaiah 9:2-7; Psalm 96; Titus 2:11-14; Luke 2:1-20

THEME IDEAS

Advent and Christmas, with their customary busyness of preparation and celebration, might make the service on Christmas Eve a welcome moment of quiet, wonder, and receiving. We hear again the story of Jesus' birth—how our savior was born as hope for peace, justice, and righteousness, for all the people of the earth. This great event is God's doing. Mary and Joseph head to Bethlehem because the Roman government demands it. The shepherds are in the field doing their job. In the midst of this ordinary human living, God, full of zealous love for humanity, comes to us.

INVITATION AND GATHERING

CENTERING WORDS *(Luke 2)*

This night we hear good news of great joy for all people.
Let us see this thing that the Lord has made known to us.

CALL TO WORSHIP *(Isaiah 9, Titus 2, Luke 2)*

All people are welcome here tonight.
We have gathered to hear the story of Jesus' birth.
All who walk in darkness,
come see a great light.
All who hope to see God,
come see the glory of our savior, Jesus Christ.
All who are simply waiting to see what's next,
come see the good news God brings.
Rejoice before God in the light and glory of this night.
We rejoice that God's grace has appeared,
bringing salvation to all.

OPENING PRAYER *(Isaiah 9, Titus 2, Luke 2)*

Holy God, help us pause in the midst of our busyness.
Quiet our minds on this Christmas Eve,
that we may hear the good news
of your gift of Jesus Christ—
your gift to a world so in need of peace,
justice, and joy.
If we walk in darkness and despair,
help us see the great light of your presence.
If we wait in hope for the coming of Christ,
help us offer hope to those around us.
Help us see your glory
breaking into our lives.
as Mary and shepherds before us saw.

In the quiet of this night,
>> may we welcome your peace and favor,
>>>> through Jesus Christ, our Messiah and Lord.
Amen.

PROCLAMATION AND RESPONSE

PRAYER OF YEARNING (Titus 2, Luke 2)

Loving God, as we celebrate the birth of your Son,
>> we yearn for light, joy, and peace
>>>> to fill our world and our lives.
We long to see your love for all people
>> in the joy of this holy night.
May we have faith like Mary and Joseph,
>> who accepted the demands of government
>>>> to travel as their child was ready to be born.
May we have faith like the shepherds,
>> who accepted God's unexpected message
>>>> and went to see God's gift with their own eyes.
May we have faith like your people throughout history,
>> who have longed to see the glory of Jesus
>>>> made manifest this holy night. Amen.

WORDS OF ASSURANCE (Isaiah 9, Luke 2)

Beloved people of God,
>> Jesus Christ has been born for us.
He is Wonderful Counselor, Mighty God,
>> Everlasting Father, Prince of Peace.
The baby lying in a manger
>> is the promise of God's peace and favor,
>> given to all.

PASSING THE PEACE OF CHRIST (Luke 2:14)

The heavenly host cry out, "Glory to God in the highest
heaven, and on earth peace!" Let us share God's peace
with one another.

INTRODUCTION TO THE WORD (Luke 2)

Let us now hear good news of great joy for all people.

RESPONSE TO THE WORD (Luke 2)

With Mary, may we treasure these words and ponder them in our hearts.

THANKSGIVING AND COMMUNION

INVITATION TO THE OFFERING (Luke 2)

After the shepherds found Mary and Joseph and the child lying in the manger, they returned to their fields, glorifying and praising God. May we too glorify and praise God for all we have seen and received as we collect tonight's offering.

OFFERING PRAYER (Isaiah 9, Titus 2)

We offer these gifts to you, Holy God,
  rejoicing that your grace has appeared
    in Jesus Christ.
May your love for all people,
  and your zeal for justice and peace,
    transform this offering into Christ's presence
      this Christmas season and always. Amen.

SENDING FORTH

BENEDICTION (Isaiah 9, Titus 2)

God's word promises us light, joy, and peace
  through the coming of Jesus Christ.
As we celebrate Jesus' birth,
  may we rejoice that it is God's passion and purpose
  to give us the kingdom.

–OR–

BENEDICTION *(Titus 2)*
The zeal of the Lord of hosts establishes God's kingdom.
May we live as God's own people,
zealous for good deeds in Jesus Christ.

December 29, 2024

First Sunday after Christmas Day

Kristiane Smith

COLOR

White

SCRIPTURE READINGS

1 Samuel 2:18-20, 26; Psalm 148; Colossians 3:12-17;
Luke 2:41-52

THEME IDEAS

The Word made flesh has come before us. Though just
boys, Jesus and Samuel found themselves in the temple
mesmerized by the teachings of the teachers and schol-
ars. They not only asked questions, they ministered to
others in their own right. Let us bring honor and praise
as we immerse ourselves in psalms, hymns and songs,
and in the teachings of Christ, the Word made flesh.

INVITATION AND GATHERING

CENTERING WORDS (Psalm 148)
May all God's messengers praise the Lord!

CALL TO WORSHIP (Psalm 148, Luke 2, Colossians 3)
> We gather this morning ready to listen.
>> **Open our ears, Lord.**
> We gather this morning ready to learn.
>> **Open our minds, Lord.**
> We gather this morning ready to love.
>> **Open our hearts, Lord.**
> We gather this morning ready to worship.
>> **Open our spirits to receive you, Lord.**
> We gather to praise the Lord Almighty!

OPENING PRAYER (1 Samuel 2, Colossians 3, Luke 2)
> Holy one, as we gather today,
>> may we be like young Jesus and Samuel—
>>> eager to hear, eager to learn,
>>>> and eager to minister to others.
> Meet us here in this sacred space.
> May our hearts and minds be open to your call,
>> as we worship and praise your holy name. Amen.

PROCLAMATION AND RESPONSE

PRAYER OF YEARNING (Colossians 3)
> God of love, we long to hear your voice,
>> but sometimes block our ears
>>> to the true words of love
>>>> you speak into our lives.
> You offer words of love and acceptance,
>> but we find reason to ignore them
>>> or withhold them from others.
> Be tolerant and forgive us in your love.
> For we yearn to find your perfect bond of unity
>> in our relationships with one another
>>> and with the world. Amen.

WORDS OF ASSURANCE (Luke 2)
When you feel like no one understands,
    sit at Christ's feet.
Ask the hard questions and listen for the answers.
God will speak.
You are not alone.
You are loved.

PASSING THE PEACE OF CHRIST (Colossians 3:13)
Called to put on compassion, kindness, humility, gentleness, and patience, let us greet one another with words
of mercy, love, and peace.

INTRODUCTION TO THE WORD (Luke 2)
As these words are read, may we hear with the eagerness of the boy, Jesus, in the Temple long ago.

RESPONSE TO THE WORD (Luke 2)
Help us hear the hard questions we need to ask.
For in asking, we discover God calling us
    into deeper relationships and greater truths.

THANKSGIVING AND COMMUNION

OFFERING PRAYER (1 Samuel 2, Luke 2, Colossians 3)
God of generosity, may your peace and your love
    seep into our hearts and our offerings,
        that we might become shining examples
            of your light in a dark and hurting world.
Thank you for your many gifts—
    this gift of community,
    the enthusiasm for learning,
    the power of generosity,
        and the gift of love.
May our gifts and our very lives
    bring your blessings to the world. Amen.

SENDING FORTH

BENEDICTION
As you leave this sacred space,
go with an excitement to share
all you have learned at the feet of Jesus.

Contributors

B. J. Beu is a UCC pastor, spiritual director, and coach who has served churches in the United Church of Christ and United Methodist Church for over twenty-five years. B. J. lives in Laguna Beach with his wife, Mary.

Michael Beu is a professional film editor, serving as the tech director for United Methodist Church of Vista, California, and worship editor for various other churches in California. www.elementproductions.net.

Mary Petrina Boyd is pastor of Marysville United Methodist Church, northeast of Seattle. She spends alternating summers working as an archaeologist in Jordan.

Joanne Carlson Brown is a retired United Methodist minister and seminary professor. She lives with Brigid, her beloved Westie.

Anna Crews Camphouse is a nurse, pastor, counselor, mom, and co-journeyer with those working to build hope and goodness in the world.

James Dollins is Senior Pastor of Anaheim United Methodist Church in Southern California, where he lives with his wife, Serena, and sons, Forrest and Silas. He is a lover of music, intercultural ministries, and God's creation.

Karin Ellis is a United Methodist pastor who lives with her husband and children in La Cañada, California. She enjoys writing liturgy for worship and children's stories.

Rebecca J. Kruger Gaudino, a United Church of Christ minister in Portland, Oregon, teaches biblical studies and theology at the University of Portland and also writes for the church.

Hans Holznagel has worked as a newspaper reporter, helped run a theater, served on the staff of a residence for low-income adults, and worked for the national ministries of the United Church of Christ in communications, mission education, administration, and fundraising. Recently retired, he and his wife, Kathy Harlow, live on Cleveland's Near West Side, where they belong to Archwood UCC.

Amy B. Hunter is a religious educator and spiritual director in Lowell, Massachusetts. She is an Episcopal layperson who loves liturgy and the occasional opportunity to preach.

Sara Dunning Lambert enjoys retired life with friends and family, especially her grandkids. She is an occasional worship leader at Bear Creek UMC in Woodinville, Washington.

Kirsten Linford serves as senior minister of Westwood Hills Congregational (UCC) church and preschool in Los Angeles. She shares her life with her young daughter, Riley, and their golden retriever, Seamus. Ecumenism is in her blood. Pastoring and parenting with a UCC head and a Disciples of Christ heart, she is delighted to be writing for a United Methodist publishing house.

Silvia Purdie is a counsellor and a minister of the Presbyterian Church of Aotearoa New Zealand. She also offers training and leadership resources for climate change and sustainability. To access her extensive collection of resources, as well as her book *Women in Creation Care,* visit www. conversations.net.nz.

Mary J. Scifres is a United Methodist pastor serving as a leadership coach, consultant, and author. Learn more at www.maryscifres.com.

Rev. Dr. Leigh Ann Shaw is an ordained elder in The United Methodist Church, who lives in Carlsbad, California. She loves writing and exploring and advocating for those without a voice.

Kristiane Smith is a United Methodist pastor serving in Southern California. Her passions include creative writing, music, hanging out with her husband and three teens, and helping others examine and make sense of their faith journey.

Leigh Anne Taylor walks alongside her husband, Hugh, and their five children and four grandchildren as a blessed "LaLa" among the clergy and churches of the Mountain View District in south central Virginia as Director of Connecting Ministries. She loves learning about the Enneagram of the Soul and spiritual practices.

Michelle L. Torigian is a pastor at St. Paul United Church of Christ in Belleville, Illinois, and blogs at michelletorigian. com. Her passions in the arts include painting and woodburning, as well as writing prayers and liturgies.

Scripture Index

Old Testament

New Testament

CPSIA information can be obtained
at www.ICGtesting.com
Printed in the USA
LVHW041211120323
741385LV00005B/7